MW00915409

Stronger Through Christ: A Mother's Memoir

Ami Dark-Rosen

Philippians 1:6

"being confident of this, that he who began a good work in you will carry it on to completion until the day of Christ Jesus." (NIV)

XULON PRESS

Copyright © 2012 by Ami Dark-Rosen

Stronger Through Christ: A Mother's Memoir
by Ami Dark-Rosen

Printed in the United States of America

ISBN 9781619964457

All rights reserved solely by the author. The author guarantees all contents are original and do not infringe upon the legal rights of any other person or work. No part of this book may be reproduced in any form without the permission of the author. The views expressed in this book are not necessarily those of the publisher.

Unless otherwise indicated, Bible quotations are taken from the New international Version. Copyright © 2011 by Biblica. Inc.

www.xulonpress.com

Philippians 4:13 "I can do all things through Christ who strengthens me."

L ife is a journey. There are many paths on the journey. There are curves, bumps, speed limits and detours. I am blessed because my path crossed Ami Dark-Rosen during our personal journeys.

We originally met over twenty years ago. She was an undergraduate student in Teacher Education and I was an instructor in the Department of Teaching at the University of Northern Iowa, Cedar Falls, Iowa. She was young, vibrant and ready to venture into her own elementary classroom to begin her teaching career. But there was a stop sign she did not expect; a stop sign that changed the direction of her life.

A physical disability forced her to continue her journey from a wheelchair. The path became more difficult with numerous obstacles. Fortunately, her internal GPS was based on her faith and in the hands of God. Proverbs 3:5-6: Trust in the LORD with all your heart and lean not on your own understanding; in all your ways submit to him, and He will direct your paths.

Ami and I had maintained a casual relationship for many years. Our paths crossed again when she relocated to live with her parents in Cedar Falls. Our friendship became closer in Cedar Falls. We were on the same path sharing the same directions and destinations. As mothers, we shared the love for our daughters. As teachers, we shared the love for education. As Christians, we shared our faith.

As you read Stronger Through Christ, you will travel down Ami's path. Her journey will touch your heart! Her path has not been easy, but through her faith and endurance she is traveling in the right direction with her destination secured. Jeremiah 29:11 "For I know the plans I have for you, 'declares the Lord,' plans to prosper you and not to harm you, plans to give you hope and a future."

Let her words touch your heart and enjoy your personal journey!

Kathy Oakland
Friend and Mentor

First of all, I want to personally thank you for purchasing this book. I am not a famous individual, but just as I believe that every person in this world has a story to tell, I wanted to share some of the most note-worthy memories in my story. This memoir includes a variety of scenarios that I have experienced in my lifetime. I started writing this in 2010, having the desire to do so for many years before. As you read these pages, I hope that you will be inspired to thank God for your life and the situations you have encountered . . . both positive and negative.

I believe that our lives are a constant reminder of the fact that this world is not our home, Heaven is our home. As you read this book, you will probably agree that this world is filled with sorrow and pain, yet He gives us the assurance that if we choose to accept Him as our personal Lord and Savior, our sins will be forgiven and our lives will be restored with Him in Paradise.

At times, my journey has seemed unbearable and full of concerns. But as a whole, my time on this Earth has proven to be joyous and filled with love and laughter. The Lord has placed many people in my life that I love. A lot of those individuals are mentioned in this book, yet there are a few who I have not included. If you are one of those people, please realize that we were in each other's lives for a reason and that God values you for the person you are. He loves all of His children and we all have a purpose.

My prayer for you is that God will continue to bless you and your loved ones, just as He has done for me.

Ami Dark-Rosen

Letter to the Reader:

June of 2010 brought an unexpected change my way; a change that permanently altered the direction of my life. I was not prepared for how to cope with how these changes would impact the remainder of my life, but I knew that the Lord would guide me through and help me to come out stronger on the other side. This memoir begins during that fated year capturing the despair and absolute sorrow I was experiencing. The chapters that follow are a snap shot of my life from the time I was five years old until the present day.

For Sarah: My Greatest God-given Gift

~~~~~~

Psalms 127:3

"Children are a heritage from the LORD,

offspring a reward from him."

(NIV)

I have written this memoir not only for myself, but as a reflection of my life for you. I want you to know more about me not only as your mom, but as you grow older, as a child who became a woman in Christ.

You will encounter times in your life when you feel scared or even angry with God, but if you stay in the Word, He will help you find your way. I want you to remember that He loves you, Sarah. I have told you this since you were a little girl. We did not become a family by coincidence, but according to His plan. You are a kind, loving, and generous person. My prayer for you is that you remain faithful to Jesus even when you are tempted to lose sight of Him. Just as I have, you will make mistakes you wish you could take back but you won't be able to do that. However, you must ask God to forgive you and don't forget to forgive yourself. When someone sins against you, forgive them as well. Most importantly, surround yourself with people who are good for your spirit and who nurture your belief in Jesus.

As you become a young woman and eventually a wife and mother, don't forget how loved you are and how God's plan for you is preparing the way for future generations to come. You are here for a purpose, Sarah. You are precious and important to Him. He died for you so you could have everlasting life in Heaven, so please do not take that for granted. You are and always will be my greatest joy in this world and when my life is

over, remember that when God is ready to call
you home, we will be reunited for Eternity!

I love you,
Mom

Chapter 1

(2010)
What Have I Done?

⎯⌇⌇⌇⌇⎯

Ephesians 2:10

"For we are God's workmanship, created in Christ Jesus to do good works, which God prepared in advance for us to do."
(NIV)

"Are you sure you didn't mean to take all of those pills?" is the question six different people asked me at the hospital two weeks ago. Every time someone different would ask the question, I would respond with the same answer.

"I was lying in bed at about eleven in the evening, trying to get my nighttime pills arranged to take before I drifted off to sleep. Because of my spinal-cord injury, I am unable to easily raise my head off the bed and actually see what I'm doing. About twenty minutes had passed by before I actually was able to swallow the medicine. My ten year old daughter was with me in the room. Since she and I only see each other every other weekend lately, I wanted to make sure that I gave her my undivided attention. I lifted the pills and instinctively poured them in my mouth." To my dismay, I'd accidentally swallowed ten of the same medicine, which was called Metoprolol (a blood pressure medicine). I quickly instructed my daughter to go get my parents, all along trying desperately to hold back the tears and concern on my face. My dad rushed me to the Emergency Room, where I continued to plead for my survival.

One of the ER nurses called Poison Control and was told that I had taken a toxic dose of my blood-pressure medicine. I could have told them that! That is why less than one minute after I swallowed the pills, I literally had to make a conscious decision to not emotionally lose it in front of my child. I knew what I had done was a mistake, but it was also very scary for her. The entire time I was in the ER, I was begging out loud to God to not take me from my daughter. Considering what our family was recently going through, I knew if I died that her faith in God may be shaken for the rest of her life. I knew she needed me now more than ever. I was afraid that if I didn't survive, she and everybody else would assume that I had taken my own life. What would that do to her? How could she ever be the person I knew God had designed her to be? Would she assume that she was responsible for my death? How would she ever forgive herself, if she did?

"Please, Jesus, don't take me now. She needs me. I want to see her live her life and selfishly, I want to see her grow up!" The thought of missing her schooling, falling in love, and having children brought immediate fear of the reality of the situation. I was desperate and it was the darkest moment of my life.

Because of His grace and mercy, my blood pressure never dropped too low. After three hours of being given IV fluids to flush toxins out quickly and drinking a couple of glasses of charcoal which was supposed to attach to the medicine in my stomach before it could be absorbed into my bloodstream, I was taken to the ICU for observation. The doctor in the ER had especially warned me about the danger of my heart rate being low enough to stop my heart. The nurse asked me if I had a Living Will on file. "I have one with my husband and my old attorney, but I need to have it updated." I just didn't have the money to pay for an attorney to do it at the time. She then asked if I wanted to be revived if my heart did stop. In spite of how inadequate I'd been feeling about my role in this world, without hesitation, I said yes.

I was released from the hospital two days later on Saturday afternoon. I went back to my parents' home where I had been living for the last three weeks. That evening, I was praying in bed, once again asking God to help me through all of the pain my daughter and I were enduring. I was asking for more blessings. It then hit me like a lightning bolt. He had given me miracles my entire life! The circumstances that had led to this point in my life were not little miracles. They had gotten me here by His design for His purpose and for His kingdom. Why wasn't I thanking Him? Once again, I neglected to honor Him for every moment of my life I had been given.

My prayer changed from begging to gratitude, shame for not realizing this earlier, strength to be strong for my child and acceptance. Thank God for that moment. It was then I realized that God has never left me and that I am here for a reason. If He was going to send me Home for Eternity, He would have done it years ago.

"What lies behind us and what lies before us are tiny matters compared to what lies within us."
Ralph Waldo Emerson

Chapter 2

(1971-1975)
What Will Define Me?

〰〰〰

Romans 8:28

"And we know that in all things God works for the good of those who love him, who have been called according to his purpose."

(NIV)

I have often wondered how my life would be different if I could alter the summer of 1976. The years that preceded 1976 could be considered as the catalyst for a challenging life to come. As I look back, I now see it as the beginning of my opportunity to mold myself into the young woman I once was and who I need to find within myself again. As I reflect on my past, present, and hopeful future, the first defining moment of my life started when I was five years old. How it would define me was up to me and my trust in God.

I think everyone of us could come up with a list of names of people in our lives who have given us roots and helped mold us in both positive and negative ways. Personally, it is not the length of each list that is important; it is the extent of the input I allow each individual to have on my life and eventual legacy I will leave for generations to come. I often wonder, "What will my daughter remember about me? Will her memories of me be filled with laughter and joy? What roots will I plant for her to build her future upon? Most importantly, what words in her mind will describe me?" I pray that one phrase she will say will be, "My mom not only was a survivor, she overcame her struggles and led by example." To be completely honest, I want to be one of the positive influences on her list, just as my mom has been for me.

How do I explain the impact my mom has had on my life? I cannot put my love and gratitude into the written word to give her the praise she deserves. I will try to lift her up, so that you may grasp a piece of what a wonderful person she is to me and those who know her.

I define my mom's devotion to me as "in-your-face "mothering." Her inability to sugar-coat over my mistakes has always been quite annoying! As I have grown older, it has been evident that she is not one to hide her true feelings with me, even when she is trying.

However, as I look back at my development as a child and how her love for me has never faltered, I see how her constant presence has been one of the most enriching influences in my life. When I hear the words "I love you" from her, there has never been any doubt in my mind that she is being completely honest with me (the same attribute that has driven me crazy)!

Mom was a divorced, single mother from the time I was less than two years old. My parents were divorced before I was two years old and my dad has been absent for most of my life. Although he was a well-liked jock in high school, let's just say that is where he peaked. The memories I have of him are so few and disappointing that it is almost humorous now. But as a little girl, it was confusing, unpredictable, and many times, filled with fear.

I am not absolutely sure what most people remember about their childhood. For me, I have certain visions in my head that particularly stand out as situations that occurred. Do I actually remember them how they really happened or is it my mind's way of protecting me from the truth? I knew for a fact that my dad was usually drunk and that his family was noticeably different than my mom's. I knew that although Mom and I were technically on our own, Grandma and Grandpa and Mom's siblings loved me and would keep me safe. I felt special and valued with them. On the other hand, Dad's family was the complete opposite.

I can remember that being with his family left me feeling isolated and like an outsider. I just never fit in.

Because of his unwillingness to pay child support (this was long before child support recovery programs were required) and the fact that he would rarely follow through with coming to visit me as scheduled, Mom was forced to protect me from his lack of commitment.

There were many times when she would get a phone call from him either the night before or hours before he was supposed to pick me up for a visit and cancel. In the 1970's, there were no cell phones and our land lines were actually attached to a wall with a cord. It is hard to believe it now, but I could hear every conversation she had as our phone was in the dining room. "Well, I guess I'll have to tell her something," I would often hear her say to him. "She's been looking forward to seeing you all week."

I never knew what he was saying to her on the other end, but I knew it was Dad and that he was not coming as promised. I assume now that he had something come up, like an opportunity to go out with someone who was probably not the best choice for him considering his "issues." I could see the concern on Mom's face. Now that I'm an adult, I know how angry she must have been at him. She was the parent who had to comfort me without influencing my feelings toward him. That must have been so hard to do. Throughout the years, I grew to develop my own beliefs and reasons to be disappointed in him. The amazing thing is that Mom never influenced me to follow her observations of the situation. What an amazing woman!

I've recently been told by individuals who know my dad that he has been sober for over three years and that his life is on the right track. Although he and I have not communicated for many years, this information makes me extremely pleased and actually very proud of him. I know that he is faced with living every day "one day at a time" and I assume that he may have many regrets concerning his lack of involvement with me during my life. I forgive him and pray that he can forgive himself. I still care about you Dad, and wish you peace and contentment.

When I think back to the first five years of my life, subconsciously I knew that Mom was my rock and that she would never abandon me. The summer of 1976 could have emotionally altered my future much worse than it actually did. This was the first defining period of my life.

"Nothing is predestined:
The obstacles of your past can become the gate-
ways that lead to new beginnings."
Unknown Author

Chapter 3

(1976)

The Diagnosis

—~~~~~~—

Luke 12:32

"Do not be afraid, little flock,
for your Father has been pleased to give
you the kingdom."

(NIV)

"Mommy, I don't feel good," were the words my mom and family heard from me many times the summer before my kindergarten year in 1976. I knew that my stomach hurt and I felt like I had the flu. I was tired all of the time.

Since Mom had no choice but to work as many hours as possible at John Deere in order to provide for us, I imagine the summer was somewhat stressful for her. When she was told by her supervisor that she was required to work overtime, she was somewhat relieved because she knew it'd be a way to earn extra money for us. However, it did not take away the fact that she and I would have limited time together during the summer.

Mom's sister and her family lived about an hour away and my aunt stayed at home with her two boys. My grandma and grandpa, who were both very loving and committed to Mom and me, lived within driving distance as well. The adults in my life decided it would be best for me to spend quite a bit of time with my extended family that summer. Although I knew that my entire family loved me, I just wanted to be with my mommy! I remember crying myself to sleep some nights and 35 years later I wonder if she was doing the same thing an hour away.

Since I was only five and my mom was an expert in not showing me her worries, I had absolutely no idea how much pain she was in from not seeing me every day of my life. She and I have always had a tight bond. The emotional pain and guilt she felt was probably unbearable for her. It would not be until years later that I would fully comprehend and experience her heartache and sacrifice.

From what I have been told, I spent most weekdays with my aunt and her family and every weekend with mom. This did not occur the entire summer, but evidently enough that I remember that detail. I do remember certain things like going camping and visiting my uncle's mom, Grandma Heaverlo. She was a kind and loving "grandma," who lived in a very old house. I can still vividly remember the smell of her home. It was musty and stale, but that did not seem to bother me because she was full of affection towards me.

Another vision in my head is the food and drinks I consumed during that summer. Because nobody knew what my eventual fate would be with my health at the time, the fact that I was always tired, excessively thirsty, and going to the bathroom all the time was not detected by my loved ones immediately. Eating Dolly Madison treats, drinking gallons and gallons of lemon aid (not Crystal Light: there were literally no sugar-free options in 1976) and other typical kid-friendly foods was not an obvious mistake at the time.

After a while, I was taken to the doctor, where my family told him about my symptoms. He obviously took a blood test, which really hurt! Okay, so I do not actually remember it being painful, but I know that I had a fear of lab draws for years to come. The doctor called and told my mom that she needed to take me to Iowa City for a consultation with an endocrinologist. His exact words were, "I'm sorry, but I think your daughter may have juvenile diabetes."

"The obstacles of your past can become the gateways that lead to new beginnings."
Author Unknown

Chapter 4

(1976)
Why am I Different?

‒‒‒‒‒‒‒‒‒‒

1 John 5:4

*"For everyone born of God
overcomes the world.
This is the victory that has overcome
the world, even our faith."*
(NIV)

The trip to Iowa City was scary for me. I knew that I was going to see doctors and that is never a good thing for a five year old to imagine. Doctors meant needles! Mom was obviously anxious too, not knowing what to expect. Iowa City Hospitals and Clinics are overwhelming places to see. Although they were not as large in 1976 as they are now, they still looked huge to me.

I can still feel the fear in my body that I felt when I first saw the doctors and nurses in their white coats carrying their clipboards. Yes, that sounds like a cliché, but that is what I can see in my mind when I recreate it in my head. They looked like giants! The head of the department was an older gentleman named Doctor Reed. I do remember him being kind to Mom and me when he told us that I was going to be admitted for a while to get my blood sugars under control. I am sure that Mom had prepared me for that reality, but hearing those words caused my stomach to drop to the floor with nerves.

I know we stayed for about one week, but little did I know that would only be the beginning of living a life with diabetes. Although they have yet to find a cure in 2012, they have learned so much more about the disease since I was diagnosed.

The one thing that has not changed is the feeling of being different than your friends when you are diabetic at a young age. We all want to feel accepted, don't we? I think if we are being honest with ourselves, we would openly admit it. The fact that I was going to be the only child in my elementary school with diabetes was not very appealing to me.

Before we were allowed to leave Iowa City, Mom and I were required to take the "Beginners Guide to Living with Diabetes" classes. I know I hated every minute of it! I knew I was missing out on things that were more fun than urine tests before every meal and snack, insulin shots in what seemed like every part of my little body, nasty tasting foods (Saccharin and Sorbital) and, of course, the things that made me burst into uncontrollable hysteria-lab draws!

I do not imagine that many young children would be very excited to see a person walk in for the first time and say, "I'm going to have to put a needle in your vein and take out some blood. It won't hurt as long as you sit still and don't be scared, OK?" I know what I was probably thinking, "Are you kidding me?"

As an adult, I can now understand the frustration of some lab techs when a child is having a tough time with the "vampires." All I have to say about that is when a child has to have labs drawn to make sure the person who is sent in at least likes children!

Mom reminds me now of the lab tech who came into my hospital room in Iowa City asking her, "Is she good with this?" and her responding, "Only if you are." You go, Mom! She was a lioness guarding her cub.

The blood draws were the scariest part of my new life with this disease, but not the most annoying. Learning how to collect my urine in a Dixie Cup was pretty much disgusting to me. The environment where I learned how to do it was a large bathroom that was, of course, dark brown (that was the popular color scheme in the 1970's), maybe six stalls with only a few having doors on them, and sinks to wash your hands (the same kind you sometimes find at an arena where someone pushes the foot pedal and the water comes out). As I think about it, it pretty much compared to a cheap dorm with a communal bathroom.

At the beginning of that week, the nurses would escort me into the group potty and stand over me in one of the stalls without a door. She would hand me the little-bitty cup and try to explain how to place the cup directly under my bottom area, so the urine would go into the plastic receptacle. Really? Not only was I supposed to pee in front of a basic stranger, there were often other nurses and kids in there at the same time putting on their brave faces. Not forgetting to mention the nasty amounts of urine that would accidentally get on my hands while trying to hit the right spot. The good thing was that by the end of my stay, the nurses trusted me enough to go in and leave my sample on my own little potty shelf. What an accomplishment.

At least the insulin shots were not so bad. (ha-ha!) I think it is one thing for a child and their family to have to gear up for an occasional flu shot, but knowing you are going to have to give yourself at least two shots a day for the rest of your life is a daunting realization for anyone. At first, the nurses would give me the shots and I hated the anxious feelings I got in my belly before breakfast and supper. Just knowing the fact that someone was going to come into my hospital room at any moment and stick a needle in my body was enough to make me lose my appetite. I am sure I had many sweet and gentle nurses who helped me during that first week, but the nurse who comes to mind is the one who looked like she was about to launch a missile into my leg or stomach. It could not have been that severe, but when you are a five year old who is already freaked out beyond belief, one's memory might be a little exaggerated.

I could not go to the next chapter without telling you about the new food choices I was told to eat. Remember, I was eating and drinking all of the things most kids ate in the mid 1970's and they all included sugar. There were no such things as Truvia, Crystal Lite, or even diet soda! There were some treats such as sugar-free candy and cookies, but they did not compare to anything else that actually tasted good to a child. Maybe it does not seem like a huge deal to most of you. Honestly as a grown woman, I now have a hard time actually remembering how out of place I felt at the time, but I can vividly recall my feelings of not being the same as my peers. I do regret not being able to understand the consequences of my actions with my diabetes until I was much older.

"The future depends on
what we do in the present."
Mahatma Gandhi

Chapter 5

(1976-1977)
The Future is yet to be Seen

~~~~~~~~~~

Philippians 2:20

"I have no one else like him, who will show genuine concern for your welfare."

(NIV)

I was discharged from the hospital in time to start my first year of school at Devonshire Elementary with the rest of the five year olds in my neighborhood. I do not recall how I felt, but I now know how nervous my mom was sending her little girl, who had recently been diagnosed with diabetes, to school for the first time. At that time, I was the only child in my school that had diabetes. I do not imagine anyone in my life was prepared for how this was going to change the course of my future and my mom's future.

The nurses had told mom to send a box of sugar cubes to school with me, leave them in the classroom, and to be prepared for a reaction. Miss Bopp was asked to keep them in the cupboard and allow me to eat one whenever I thought my blood sugar was low.

Evidently, I must have had a lot of lows my first few weeks of kindergarten because my mom got a telephone call from Miss Bopp telling her that I was constantly asking for sugar! Duh... What five year old is not going to use that to get attention and sugar? I actually think it is a little funny now. But I do not think Miss Bopp did.

One particular story my mom tells me is of the time when I got home from school and my babysitter, who happened to have diabetes as well, noticed that I was weak and my body was shaking. Mom later found out that Miss Bopp had sent me home with a low blood sugar. Although most of the neighbor kids walked home together, it was still about six or seven blocks to our house. I would like to give Miss Bopp the benefit of the doubt, but my guess is that she assumed I was faking another reaction. I have thought about what could have happened in the worst-case scenario. I could have passed out; my friends would not have known what to do since diabetes was so new for me, and I could have eventually gone into a diabetic coma!

Thank God that never happened. It was not just a coincidence that my babysitter, named Georgia, was also diabetic. It was not a matter of luck that I did not lose consciousness before I made it to Georgia's either. I believe with everything inside of me that it was Jesus Christ protecting me.

By the time summer came around again, most of my friends and their parents knew about my diabetes. As a child, I hated that! I could not get away with anything! If I got away with sneaking a treat without any adult knowing, my friends would always end up tattling on me. That was my perspective at the time.

One example I can remember was in the summer between first and second grade. Georgia was my full-time babysitter during the summer since Mom had to work her normal hours. Georgia's family lived next door, so it was convenient for all of us. All of the kids in our neighborhood were allowed to play all day as long as they checked in at home every once in a while. So, of course, my check-in spot was at Georgia's. She and her husband had three boys of their own. Joel, their middle son, and I would often spend time together in the neighborhood. He was a few years younger and I remember that there were times when Georgia would "encourage" me to let Joel come along with me to my friends' houses.

One hot summer day, Joel and I went looking for something to do. Since I was the experienced elder of the two of us, I knew the hot spots where there would be lots of kids around to play with. We walked to Kris's, Tony's, and goodness knows where else. Nobody was home. Our last resort was to stop at Michelle's. Michelle did not have many friends. Unfortunately, I was sometimes a part of making her feel left out with the kids in our neighborhood and school. I have since felt shame for inflicting emotional pain on her.

As I got older, I realized how awful it was of me to do that to another person. Like many girls, I wanted to be accepted by the popular girls. Part of making that happen for me was showing off to those girls by feeling powerful over someone weaker than me, like Michelle.

The most prevalent thing I remember about her was that none of the kids in the neighborhood were ever allowed to enter her house. If I went to her house to ask if she could play or hang out, I had to wait outside while her mom hollered for her to come out. This happened no matter what the weather was doing outside: rain, snow, ice, or extreme Iowa humidity. Unfortunately, I now wonder if her family was experiencing something personal, which could have caused shame or embarrassment for Michelle.

That summer day, Joel and I stopped at Michelle's. Her mom invited us in for warm, chocolate-chip cookies. I decided to take full advantage of the situation! It was not just an opportunity to spy on Michelle's family, but a golden opportunity to eat cookies without Georgia or my mom finding out. In my mind, I thought, "Joel won't tell his mom because he doesn't even realize that I shouldn't be eating sweets."

Joel could not have been older than four or five at the time and I was very confident that it would never be shared with anyone. Since Michelle's mom seemed like a recluse to me, I naturally assumed that she would not tell either. That proved to be false confidence. We stayed at Michelle's for as long as it took to consume countless amounts of scrumptious, gooey cookies. Afterwards, our stomachs were full of carbohydrates packed with sugar. Conveniently for Joel's mom, Georgia, we heard her calling our names for lunch. Although I felt like my stomach was going to explode, I knew I was going to have to fake that I was starving!

We walked to Joel's house. The entire time I was planning how to avoid the inevitable. Remember, Joel really had no idea about the word "diabetes," so my plans did not include prepping him on how to cover-up my cheating. I realized that if I was "famished" because of how hard we had played all morning, then Georgia would never suspect that I had just consumed at least a handful of sugary treats. I can remember being nervous because I knew I would have to eat a lot of lunch! I am not able to recall what she served, but I do vividly recall asking for seconds.

I was so busy stuffing my little, guilty face that I was not aware that Joel had not touched his lunch. The last thing I remember about that meal is Georgia asking Joel why he was not eating lunch. To my surprise, he answered by saying, "I'm not hungry. Ami and I ate a whole bunch of yummy, chocolate chip cookies at Michelle's right before we came home." Since Georgia was a responsible adult, she did what any other neighborhood parent would have done. She called Michelle's mom to confirm.

"When you can't change the direction
of the wind — adjust your sails."
H. Jackson Brown

Chapter 6

(1977)
A Mother and Daughter's Love

—⁓⁓⁓⁓—

Colossians 1:13
"For he has rescued us from the dominion of darkness and brought us into the kingdom of the Son he loves"
(NIV)

A child who has been diagnosed with diabetes at such a young age can spend countless days in hospitals, feeling lonely, scared, and confused. I cannot recall how many actual days I was hospitalized, but I would imagine they add up to many months.

One particular memory occurred in the cold, winter months of 1976. My mom and I were living in our little ranch home and Mom was scheduled to be at work at 6:00 in the morning. It was still dark and snowy outside when Mom woke me up at 5:30 to get me ready to go to the babysitter's. When she came into my room and was rubbing my back to wake me, she realized that I was unable to speak or move the right side of my body. As she struggled to get my clothes on my body, my arm and leg were literally flopping on the bed. She remembers that the look on my face was one of absolute fear and that I was unaware of what was happening to me. Mom's friend, Colleen, was on the way to pick her up for work. While we waited, Mom tried to feed me something, hoping that it would make me feel better. I can still envision myself laying in my mom's lap with my eyes directly on her looking for reassurance. She gave me the peace in my heart just by her soft voice humming a lull-a-bye and telling me that she loved me.

When we arrived at the hospital, I was swiftly taken to the Emergency Room. It did not take them long to inform my mom that I had just endured a stroke. As they continued to provide interventions, Mom went to the church chapel to pray for my healing. Mom then decided to call her parents who lived over 1 ½ hours away, and they immediately jumped into their car to join her at the hospital.

By the time Grandma and Grandpa arrived, the doctors had already informed my mom that they believed that they had been mistaken about my diagnosis. After more intensive testing, they changed their diagnosis and believed that I had actually suffered a terrible low-blood sugar. My body somehow recovered and by the time I was discharged from the hospital (one week later) I was back to my normal self.

The thoughts I had at that time and during future instances at hospitals are challenging to accurately describe. I now realize how grateful I am for God always restoring my health so that I could live a typical childhood. As I have witnessed others during my lifetime (particularly children) who do not survive, I thank Him for allowing me to continue in this world.

However, when I was a young girl, who was in the hospital for days-on-end and my mom was not always able to spend the evenings with me because of her job, I often cried myself to sleep. The room would always seem so very dark and scary and I knew in my heart that I felt alone. On the contrary, the noises throughout the hall-ways and at the nurse's station were so loud that I felt as if I was in the middle of a gymna-sium surrounded by hundreds of people.

The best days at the hospital were usually the ones where I would be well enough to be allowed to go into the children's play room to paint, read, listen to music, or hang out with the other kids who had been there at the same time and were just as lonely as I was. Of course, my absolute favorite part of any hospital stay was coming home to Mom and often my Grandma and Grandpa who had travelled to our home to lavish me with love.

"If you have a mom, there is nowhere you are likely to go where a prayer has not already been."
Robert Brault

Chapter 7

(1982)
What in the World was I Thinking?

~~~~~~~~~~~~

Luke 7:13

"When the Lord saw her,

his heart went out to her and

he said, "Don't cry."

(NIV)

C hildhood is oftentimes filled with laughter, friendships, and innocence concerning the evil forces that surround us. When I look back at that time of my life, I recall memories and sometimes can envision the actual moments that made those memories.

I can see vivid, colorful pictures of occasions such as preparing for a dance recital every spring after months of hard work and preparation. Tap and jazz dance were huge outlets for me. I have never been talented in sports of any kind and have always been embarrassed by my lack of skill. I use the term "skill" loosely because that word implies that I had something to work with. Well, not so much! Dancing, on the other hand, was something I did well and always enjoyed. I was the student who all the other girls in my class would turn to for questions and advice about how I did certain moves and steps. It gave me a feeling of empowerment and pride to be able to help my friends in my group feel good about their performance.

My mind is also full of sweet memories of experiences with my extended family, including aunts, uncles, and of grandparents. There are far too many situations to share with you, but since both of my grandparents are now with their Heavenly Father, I need to honor them by including a few very strong memories. My grandparents loved all of their children and grandchildren equally, but I believe that they both sensed how much they meant to me. I spent a lot of time at their home when I was younger and they strived to help me feel valued and important in their lives. They accomplished this by not only their affirming words but also their actions towards me. For example, my grandpa made an effort to show interest in my life and the things that I had passion for like dance, music, school, and friends. He and Grandma made it a point to attend every activity I was involved in, no matter the time or place. I am taking a wild guess here, but my grandpa in particular deserves a lot of credit for this since he was a man who was passionate about "manly" things such as fishing and machinery.

My grandma showed her unconditional love towards me in her own unique ways. She had always sewn clothing for her family and continued that for me when I was a child until I became an adult. Her creations were absolutely beautiful. I was honored to wear the items that she made for me. She would always put a personal touch in the outfits by sewing a tag on the inside which said, "Made with Love by Grandma."

My grandparents also made a point to do the little things to let me know how much I meant to them. For example, I desired to have my hair French braided for the first day of school in third grade. They drove to our home from 1 ½ hours away so Grandma could do my hair so that I felt pretty for third grade.

Another aspect of my life I felt proud of were my accomplishments in school. I certainly was not the smartest kid in my grade and had to work very hard to excel. I did love school! I have always enjoyed a challenge and accomplishing goals. I believe this was instilled in me by my mom at an early age. I did not realize it at the time, but watching her get up early every morning and go to work, come home, and take care of the house (impeccably, I might add) was an amazing example of follow-through and grit.

My desire to do well was not only focused on myself but others too. Although that sounds noble, it came along with instances where I was bossy or demanding towards my friends. As I previously mentioned, one of my main desires was to "fit in" with the popular girls. However, the term, "popular" has an entirely different meaning to me now than it did during my childhood.

Just as it does today, "popular" usually referred to the kids who were attractive to others and seemed to have a sense of who they were. This did not indicate that they were necessarily kind people, but that they knew where they belonged in relation to other kids. The mean girls KNEW they were mean and owned it! Never in my mind did I intend to be a mean person but my desire to fit in occasionally swayed me to treat others unkindly. When I felt inspired to help a friend with dance class, schoolwork, or even playing a game, my initial words of encouragement would sometimes turn into harsh or bossy tones.

Unfortunately for my mom, one example still resonates in both our minds which demonstrated my keen ability to feel empowered by "helping others." I am referring to an incident when I was in 3rd grade. My friend Amy had invited me to her slumber party to celebrate her birthday. Many other friends from our class were there and it was a great night for all. Her mom had prepared a multitude of activities such as singing in the microphone to music, Twister (the game), a scavenger hunt in the neighborhood, and, of course, cake and lots of treats! Just as my mom had done at every party I had been invited to in the past, she had given Amy's mom instructions about what I was allowed to eat. She also sent along options for alternatives for me: fruit, pretzels, chips, granola bars. Yummy! Hopefully, you are able to sense my sarcasm in that word!

As I think about it now, it makes perfect sense why the following "teaching moment" occurred. Amy's party was incredible. The only thing that I thought could improve it was to conduct a lesson on how to give an insulin shot. What in the world was I thinking? Obviously, I did not need to learn how to give myself a shot, because I had already been doing that for years. But the other girls certainly needed their own lessons. This is what was going through my mind at the time. I do not remember which young lady was nominated to be my guinea pig. I can only imagine her fear while I respectfully and professionally explained how I was going to give her a shot of water through my B-D syringe. Knowing what I know now, I thank God that I did not use insulin! God only knows how tragically that could have turned out.

I placed the needle on my friend's arm, while calming her nerves with my soft voice. In other words, I did not want the other girls to know what was happening in the bathroom. "It's going to be just fine. I do this all the time at home and it doesn't even hurt," I said, as I prepared her for the "little stick." As fast as lightening, she broke free of my gentle grasp, threw the door open, and screamed to the other girls, "Ami just tried to give me one of her shots!"

Obviously, my explanation of that occurrence is somewhat "exaggerated for effect," but it is definitely true. Why did I do that horrible thing to that young girl who was my friend? Why did the thought even enter my mind? I still cannot answer that. I do know that I felt different than the other girls at the party; they could eat all the cake and ice cream they wanted. They did not have to do a urine test and self-administer an insulin shot before they ate. Everyone else there came from a two-parent home with siblings and spoke of their brothers and sisters that night. Who knows? I knew I was missing something that I did not have.

"It is never too late to be what

you might have been."

George Eliot

Chapter 8

(1977-1983)
Hertko Hollow

〰〰〰

2 Corinthians 7:10

"Godly sorrow brings repentance that leads
to salvation and leaves no regret,
but worldly sorrow brings death."

(NIV)

There was one advantage to becoming diabetic - Camp Hertko Hollow. Hertko Hollow was a week-long summer camp for kids with diabetes. It was something I looked forward to every summer during the school year. At camp, diabetic kids were nurtured by YMCA counselors and teenage counselors who also had the disease. It was the perfect set-up!

Hertko Hollow had every activity for the imag-
inations of all of us: swimming, archery, horse-
back riding, arts-and-crafts, canoeing, and
much more. We were allowed to make our own
schedules for what we wanted to do. Since the
camp was designed for us to walk everywhere,
all we had to do was walk from one activity to
another and sign up. I loved and kind of feared
the horse barn, so I made sure to sign up every
day for that.

The camp was designed to teach us the importance of taking care of ourselves, so a lot of activities centered on our urine tests or blood sugars,
insulin shots, four basic food groups, and physical activity. And, we were often rewarded for
making healthy choices and there were always
fun prizes given out to campers when we accomplished something new. One such award was
called the Belly Buster and was designated for
the campers who gave their own insulin shots
in their stomach for the first time.

The songs, campfires, dining hall, and camp store provided me with hours of entertainment. I am including the camp store in that statement because of the time it took me to choose my items. I loved the idea of doing my own "shopping." We were allowed to purchase anything we wanted throughout the day including craft projects, T-shirts, sugar-free soda (Tab or Fresca), and sugar-free goodies. It was probably 1979 or so when the camp store first offered Velemints candy. I believe it was one of the first sugar-free candies on the market at the time so all of us diabetic kids were thrilled to actually be able to buy candy at the store. Yeah, it was just a sugar-free mint, but to us it was like hitting the jackpot! Since we were allowed to buy as many items as our little hearts desired, I know I personally bought at least two packages of the scrumptious "desserts" a day for the first few days of camp. Most of the girls in my cabin had done the same and there were approximately 12-15 cabins throughout the camp.

Remember that this particular candy was one of the "Charter Members" of sugar-free candies, so naturally the sweetener used was called Sorbital. I am assuming it is no longer used because of the nasty aftertaste it left in your mouth and the fact that sweeteners have now evolved into options like Stevia and others. Back in the days of Sorbital, there were often side effects that were not very pleasant if someone digested too much of those particular ingredients. For example, over 150 kids at camp eating an average of 20 mints per day for 6 days! Did I forget to mention the nasty side-effects? Diarrhea! Oh, the poor camp counselors.

Although camp allowed me to be surrounded by other kids with the same health issues as I had and it was a perfect time to learn coping skills from one another, I personally picked up on some "hints" that were harmful. There were teenaged girls at camp who had ways to get attention from boys that were extremely unhealthy and irresponsible. These young women would purposefully give themselves too much insulin which would cause them to have a low-blood sugar. Some of these girls would be guaranteed to have a reaction and would "desperately need" a teenage boy to carry them to the dining hall or nurse for juice or sugar of some kind.

On the other extreme, there were rumors around camp of girls who would intentionally choose to not give themselves insulin. You may be wondering why? I was curious about that too, so I asked around and found out that if a diabetic did not take their insulin, then they would eventually lose weight. That sounded appealing to me. I had never been overweight, but I was far from thin either. As I look back at my younger pictures, I was just the right weight for a girl my age and height. I just wish I believed that at the time. That would have made a huge impact on my future. It must have been one of my last years of going to camp when I heard about the "diabetic diet plan." I was old enough to know that I wanted to try it for myself. It makes me very sad to admit that one of the best memories of my childhood, Camp Hertko Hollow, is also where I was introduced to and chose to partake in such a detrimental and dangerous skill.

I spent many years experimenting with my insulin and using that tactic as a rapid-weight loss plan. This did cause me to be able to stay very thin but the long-term detrimental effects it left on my body will always be one of my greatest regrets. You will gain an understanding of what I did to my body and how it has affected almost every aspect of my life. I am extremely disappointed in myself for causing the pain to not only myself, but my family, friends, and of course, to God. Our bodies are supposed to be treated as a temple and I took advantage of His gift to me - my life.

However, I remember that He forgives me and that He has taken my regrets and turned them into many beautiful outcomes for me and my loved ones. I must always rely on the fact that He knows how far it is from the east to the west.

Our lives are comparable to a huge puzzle. Each piece being strategically put in place is designed by God, only God! We are only capable of seeing individual pieces, where He sees the entire, completed masterpiece even before we were born. Now, that is encouraging, don't you agree?

"It is not because things are difficult that we do not dare; it is because we do not dare that things are difficult."

Seneca

Poster child will ride bike to raise funds

Amy McCormick will ride in the Diabetes Bike Ride Sunday to raise funds for the programs of diabetes research, education, detection and summer camp for diabetic youth.

Her reason for riding is personal—she has diabetes. For this perky, 8-year-old blonde there is the sobering realization that for her, without the bike ride and other fund-raising efforts to support research, she may have to live her entire life depending on daily injections of insulin.

To sustain life, she will face the many complications associated with the disease such as blindness, kidney failure and many others. Amy has been diabetic since she was five.

DIABETES has the distinction of being the "hidden disease." About 10 million Americans have diabetes, more than 140,000 in Iowa. Diabetes is the leading cause of all new cases of blindness in the country and the third leading cause of death by disease.

The American Diabetes Association, Iowa Affiliate Inc. began funding research at the University of Iowa in 1976. More than $400,000 for the research has been raised through bike rides.

In addition to the bike ride in the Waterloo-Cedar Falls area, rides will be conducted in Waverly, Traer and 19 other cities in Iowa.

Amy McCormick   Courier photo by Jeneanne

I was the Iowa Diabetic Poster Child during the years of 1979 & 1980, ages 8 and 9.

Chapter 9

(1982)
The Longing for a Family

~~~~~~~~

Romans 12:10

"Be devoted to one another in love. Honor one another above yourselves." (NIV)

Being an only child with a life-long disease seemed unbearable at times. I am fully aware that many children do very well as only children, but my experience with knowing both scenarios has been so enriching that I would choose to have siblings if I were given a choice. There were times when my friends were too busy to play and those days were lonely ones. During the school day, my world was the same as the other kids in my class: filled with friends, recess, hot lunches, and such. But the evenings and summer times were another story. Although Mom did an amazing job organizing my schedule to allow me to stay active, a single parent can only be expected to do so much. That is why I was so incredibly blessed to have Hank Dark come into our lives. My mom worked at John Deere in Waterloo, Iowa during my entire childhood. She had dated a couple of very nice men but because she was always looking out for me which I now realize as an adult, she was very cautious about whom she allowed in our home. She never introduced me to anyone who did not end up having a friendship with me and who respected my mom and me. Because I trusted her with that assurance, I knew that when she first mentioned Hank Dark to me and explained who he was, I think I automatically knew that he was going to end up being very important to both of us.

At the time, Hank was employed at John Deere as a Supervisor in the Employee

Assistance Program. His job was multi-faceted, ranging from working with the Alcohol Anonymous program to putting on seminars with John Deere employees. Mom initially met him during a required seminar at Deere which she and the other employees in her department were required to attend. She was just a random person in the room listening to Hank speak, when she decided to ask him to meet with her to discuss the best ways to help me deal with feeling abandoned by my father. She met with Hank a few times before she invited him to our home to talk with me. To this day, I still laugh at the first words I said to him, "No offense, but do you know how short you are?" Trust me when I say that I had no room to talk!

Oh! I am so sorry Dad. Hank Dark later married my mom and adopted me a year later. From now on in this memoir, I refer to Hank Dark as "dad" because he is the only dad I have ever really known. He has been a wonderful leader of our family and I honor him for his service to me and our entire family. Dad, I know there are times when you have felt as if you have not been able to fulfill your dreams. For that, I am sorry. Without you, I would not be the person I am today. Your unconditional love and respect for me is what has made me the woman I am today. You are loving and kind and I am grateful for you coming into my life. Thank you for being you!

Dad had two children from a previous marriage: Beth and Michael. We have been a tight-knit family since 1982. I love my family more than words can say. In fact, people usually had no knowledge that we were even a blended family unless we brought it to their attention. There were times when individuals would ask my mom or dad, "Now, which ones are yours?" meaning, which of the kids were either of their biological children. We would privately take great offense at that question because we just always considered ourselves as a typical family. Genetics meant nothing to us. We loved one another from the beginning and it has never failed us. Mom and Dad's typical response to that question was, "They're all ours, but thank you for asking."

Beth is three years younger than I. She and I became not only sisters but friends, almost immediately. We have made countless memories together in college, church mission trips, side-by-side work at Village Inn and Applebee's Restaurants, and now raising our children together. She has always been one of my best friends and as an adult she is an excellent source of spiritual strength for me. I love you Beth. I love and appreciate that I am Katherine, Anne, and Luke's aunt. I am honored to be your sister.

My little-brother Michael is more like a big brother to me. As he has grown older, he has become quite a man, taking on the responsibility of not only being a wonderful husband to my dear sister-in-law, Angie, and an amazing father to my hilariously funny niece Reese and equally as entertaining nephew Landon (Buddy). He is also learning how to be a next-generation leader of our extended family. Michael, I love you for the memories we have created together in our childhood and for your continued commitment to honor, integrity, and character that all men should possess. You are an amazing person Michael and I am proud of the man you have become.

I am grateful for my family and the fact that when the Lord calls me home (hopefully many years from now), those memories will be shared for many generations to come. God definitely knew exactly what He was doing when He sent Mom to listen to Hank Dark speak at that John Deere Seminar in 1982. God is good all the time!

"Family faces are magic mirrors.
Looking at people who belong to us,
we see the past, present, and future."
Gail Lumet Buckley

Chapter 10

(1983-1994)
When Life was so Much Easier

—⟨⟨⟨⟨⟩⟩⟩⟩—

Colossians 4:2

"Devote yourselves to prayer, being watchful and thankful."

(NIV)

I decided to keep the experiences about my junior high, high school, and college years very brief because the fact is that the only true thing I can share with you is that those years were wonderful! There were the normal situations filled with drama, tears, boys, friends, etc., but as a whole, I generally smile when I think of those situations. They helped to mold me into the person I am today and remind me of the days when life was not full of "real-world" concerns. The main memories I have are of particular teachers and experiences which are filled with laughter and joy, band trips, football games, pom pon competitions, choir, friendships, church youth group trips, and so forth.

Of course, one of the defining moments in my life was meeting my fiancé in our education classes while we both attended the University of Northern Iowa. I had never felt as if I was in love before and it was a wonderful shock and surprise to meet him during our last year at UNI. He was in a Fraternity and since I was a member of Alpha Delta Pi Sorority, we were able to spend quite a bit of time together the last two semesters of college. We were engaged only six months after we met and I believed that we would be together forever through good times and bad, in sickness and health, till death do us part. Our whirlwind relationship would soon encounter a serious curveball that we would have to learn how to navigate through and hopefully come out stronger on the other side.

"We all have our time machines.
Some take us back, they're called memories.
Some take us forward, they're called dreams."
Jeremy Irons

Chapter 11

(1994)
Homer's First Team

=~~~~~~~

1 Thessalonians 5:18
"Give thanks in all circumstances; for this is God's will for you in Christ Jesus."
(NIV)

I mmediately after our UNI graduation, my fiancé and I travelled to Texas interviewing for teaching positions. We acknowledged that it would be a challenge for both of us to be hired in the same school in Iowa since teaching jobs in Iowa were extremely difficult to obtain. We desired to be in close proximity to one another for emotional support. We also had the desire to start off on our own and not need to rely on our families as much as we had. To tell you the truth, I never really wanted to move to Texas. I have always been so close with my entire family and I knew I would be terribly home-sick. I also accepted that I would have to start making necessary sacrifices for my new mar-riage. Texas is a great, beautiful state! I love taking vacations there, but I am an Iowa girl through-and-through.

We had an amazing time in Texas. We inter-viewed as planned, but did some sight-seeing and a lot of eating at local restaurants. I can remember going to a few authentic Mexican res-taurants and totally salivating thinking about the warm chips and fresh guacamole. The most memorable meal we had was on the Gulf of Mexico; it consisted of fresh seafood. I love sea-food and had not had the "real thing" since I was a child when my family and I would travel to Oklahoma and Texas to visit my dad's family.

The restaurant was also romantic, although it was hotter than the sun and humid beyond belief. It was still gorgeous. We had been traveling all day after interviewing the day before and wanted to spend one of our last evenings enjoying ourselves. I do not remember exactly what I ate, but I am sure part of my meal was shrimp (I love them).

I will never forget one of the items, raw oysters. My fiancé was so anxious for me to try one because he had previously been to Italy and thought they were delicious. I remember saying, "Are you kidding me? These look disgusting. I'm not eating these slimy things!"

"Oh, come on. That way you can go home and tell people you ate fresh Gulf oysters." So, I threw my head back and swallowed one, very reluctantly, I might add. Trust me; I will never do that again. The rest of the evening was enjoyable, watching and listening to the waves come in and then leaving the shore. It was magical.

The next day we jumped in the little car we had borrowed from my mom to drive on the long trip and headed back to Iowa. We were thrilled because we both felt positive about our interviews and were hopeful for our up-and-coming future. This was May of 1994 and our wedding was planned for September of that year. Now that I think about it, I am not sure what we would have done if things had gone as planned because school started before September and we were getting married in Cedar Falls, Iowa. Once again, God was directing His plan, not ours.

We got back to Iowa and went back to our daily routines waiting for a call from Texas for a job offer. I was a server at Applebee's Restaurant and my fiancé had a job at a hardware store. We thought we were the busiest people that had ever existed. We were planning a wedding, saving money for our potential move to another state, going out with friends (priorities, you realize) and enjoying our new relationship. We anxiously awaited a telephone call from any Texas school administrator. Finally, I received one. "Ami, this is (I don't remember her name) from Rosenberg

Consolidated School District. We'd like to informally offer you an elementary-teaching position at one of our elementary schools for the 1994-1995 school year. However, we need you to complete one additional step in the process which is a short telephone interview."

I do not remember what my actual response was at that time, but I would not doubt if it contained some stuttered words. I was shocked because I had not been expecting this by any means! But I did it and I believe I did pretty well, because I was told that things looked promising and to be expecting a phone call.

During the month of June, we also travelled to Illinois to interview for teaching jobs. I was much more excited for these interviews because it was not so far away from Iowa. I felt very positive about this experience as well and actually received a tentative offer from Pekin Community School District depending on how many of their teaching staff were either going to retire or transfer to another building. I was thrilled!

However, I started feeling extremely ill during the month of June. It started with aches and pains and progressed to unbearable pain in my neck and shoulders. To this day, I have never been in so much agony. I had a fever of over 103 degrees, could barely move my body, and eventually had to call in sick at Applebee's on the Fourth of July. I had worked all through high school and college all along involved in band, choral, poms, church, sorority activities, amongst other activities. I had hardly missed a day of work because of sickness. So for my sister to actually have to make the phone call to our manager was very odd.

From that point on, I do not remember much of the summer of 1994, but I do remember walking myself into the Emergency Room of Satori Memorial Hospital. Satori is a wonderful hospital, with many caring nurses, doctors, and other staff. However, it is a smaller facility and since it was a holiday weekend, many doctors themselves were on vacation. The remainder of this chapter and the one following are all memories given to me from my family and friends as I have limited memories of that time in my life.

Since my fever was so high for an adult and I had such pain my neck and shoulders, two spinal taps were done to check for meningitis. I do recall being extremely anxious with them sticking needles in my spine, but do not remember what it actually felt like. I do not even recall if it hurt.

I have been told that I eventually lost consciousness because my stats were looking very grim. My blood pressure was evidently going out-of-control and I had swelled up like a balloon. The nurses could not locate any viable veins for blood draws. My oxygen levels were dangerously low and they feared for my life.

My parents called our pastor Homer Larsen. He came to pray over me with my family. I would love to recite the actual prayer here but it obviously is not remembered by anyone. I can guarantee that it was heartfelt and that the Lord heard Homer. I have been told by those in my hospital room that my eyes opened for the first time in three days when Homer was praying. We were surrounded by the hospital staff and many family and friends who had evidently heard about my failing health and came to the hospital to pray and support my immediate family.

The physicians at Satori discovered that I had what is called multi-systems failure which is defined by the liver, kidneys, and lungs all failing simultaneously. My body was shutting down and they knew that there was infection in my body yet they could not determine the source of it. My fiancé had been out of town interviewing and visiting his family. Before I had lost consciousness, I had asked my sister to call him and tell him that I was undergoing some testing but not to worry. As I recall, I remember that I did not want to concern him with my health and subsequently affect his job interview. I think (knowing myself) that I was probably so excited for him to possibly be finding a teaching job, I did not want his mind to be pre-occupied with me at the time.

The hospital staff at Satori, although very competent, felt helpless because it was out of their capabilities at their small facility. My parents asked Homer for his advice because somehow along the way Saint Mary's Hospital in Rochester had been mentioned. Homer looked at Mom and Dad and said, "Mayo has always been my first-team."

"So do not fear, for I am with you;
do not be dismayed, for I am your God. I will
strengthen you and help you; I will uphold you
with my righteous right hand."
The Holy Bible-Isaiah 41:10 (NIV)

Chapter 12

(1994)
God's Mercy Revealed

―~~~~~~―

Proverbs 28:13

"Those who conceal their sins do not prosper, but those who confess and renounce them find mercy."

(NIV)

Once I became unconscious and unable to respond to stimuli, the staff at Satori and my parents made a decision that saved my life. Within one hour of being told that I would not survive at the rate in which my health continued to worsen, I was taken to Mayo's emergency room in Satori's helicopter. I obviously do not recall anything about the trip but my family was later told that I barely survived it. My stats continued to plummet and the wonderful flight-nurse with me worked non-stop to keep me alive until we landed. The amount of actual time it takes from Cedar Falls, Iowa to Rochester, Minnesota in the helicopter is only thirty-forty minutes. Because of the male nurse who happened to be working that particular shift on the 4th of July, my life was spared. I have much gratitude for him.

I can only imagine the panic my parents, my sister and brother, my aunt and uncle, who were there for my arrival, and fiancé, endured as they frantically jumped in their vehicles and followed the helicopter. The Lord was many places that evening holding many hands. He guided my family to the hospital safely and was with me, the nurse, and the pilot every step of the way.

When I arrived on the helicopter holding pad at Mayo, things evidently became even more precarious for me. Mayo had been notified ahead of time about our arrival and was equally prepared. From what I have been told, I could not even leave the landing pad for forty-five minutes while the Chief of Staff of St. Mary's Hospital amongst other professionals stabilized me enough to be able to be moved in any fashion.

Once I was stable enough to be taken to the Critical Intensive Care Unit, things did not improve. My entire extended family, my fiancé's family, Homer, and many close-family friends eventually made their way to Rochester. The doctors could not determine the cause of my sudden illness nor source of the infection. After undergoing many MRI's, CAT Scans, and the multiple arterial lines throughout my body (including my neck-yuck), countless numbers of additional intravenous lines, and goodness knows what else, they decided to perform a tracheotomy, so that I could receive enough oxygen to survive. Since it had already been determined that I had multi-systems failure, they were aware that my life, if it was spared, would never be the same. Basically, every organ in my body, except my heart, had shut down. Just the fact that I am here today to share my story is a testament to our glorious, merciful Savior.

My family watched me for the next eight weeks fight the battle of my life. There were days where it seemed as if I were improving. The first day that my chance of survival percentage moved above zero percent, my family had a celebration in the family waiting room. When the doctor entered the room and exclaimed, "She's above zero!" they went to the grocery store and purchased a cake. That makes me chuckle now because I know my family's sense of humor and that they were desperately trying to stay positive and grateful to God for sparing my life at that time.

My parents explain this time as a surreal time in their lives. They spent twelve to sixteen hours a day with me in my hospital room or near the St. Mary's campus with the fear of being too far away from me. At the beginning, they had been told that I had a ten-day window for survival.

This meant that the first ten days were crucial to my future chances to live. If I did not make it past the first ten days, chances were that I would not survive at all. If you are a parent, I am sure you literally cannot imagine their fear.

Once I made the eleventh day without losing my life, the doctors were obviously relieved. They explained to my parents that I was not even close to being "out of the woods." In fact, they gave them the following visual to help them understand the magnitude of my health concerns. They told Mom and Dad that my chance of success was like carrying sixteen eggs in your arms at the same time without being able to drop one. If one dropped, then it would possibly be fatal.

My mom recalls the scariest moment of the situation for her when the neurologist discovered my pupils changing sizes. They noticed that they would often become enlarged and then eventually return to their normal size. They were unable to determine the cause of the problem. They explained to my parents that the dilation of my eyes could be caused by the infection spreading to my brain. My mom was understandably worried for her daughter and wondered if I would ever be able to function as I had before this troublesome news. She started to question God and why He would allow such a horrible thing to happen to her child. But He comforted her and with many more mercies. He spoke words of hope to her and comforted her in her time of grief and fear.

To make matters worse, while they were performing the various tests on my body, the doctors found something that worried them about my recovery (if there was going to actually be a recovery was yet to be determined) and they decided to share their concern with my parents.

While the doctors were probably sad to tell my mom and dad the situation they had discovered, they pulled my parents aside and showed them the actual scan that showed that I had a blocked carotid artery. To the healthcare team, it looked as if I had a stroke while in the coma. My mom and dad were stricken with grief and sorrow wondering what that would mean for my future. They questioned the doctors which led them to reinvestigate the films that showed the damage. They came to the conclusion that the blocked carotid had occurred when I was much younger like maybe six-years old? Mom then explained to them about the experience we had when I was a little girl and how the physicians had initially believed that I had had a stroke but then changed their diagnosis. The team at St. Mary's were amazed and very intrigued which led them to consult the neurologist who explained that what had probably happened was that my body had compensated when I was younger. This tricked my brain into allowing the other side of my body to take over the function of the side which had been affected. He followed up the conversation by telling them that this does not occur for adults but only in young children. How lucky can I be? It is not luck. It is He who has given me countless blessings along my path.

The Lord continued to stay faithful, steadfast, and present every moment of my three months at St. Mary's. He guided the doctors, nurses, and professional staff's hands. He kept my family hopeful and focused on my success. He was merciful and present even in the darkest hours.

People have asked me if I remember anything about my six weeks in the coma. The answer is no. I have even joked about the conversation God and I could have had during my days when I was not aware of my surroundings:

"My child, I'm not bringing you home with me quite yet. You have not fulfilled my plans for you. I'm giving you more time to learn more about me and your purpose."

"Thank you, Heavenly Father. Besides, I just got engaged, graduated from college, and have my life ahead of me."

We all know that probably did not happen but one thing I am assured of is that Jesus was with me holding my hand. He was whispering words of love and peace in my ear. I do believe that He allowed me to stay on Earth to fulfill His plans for me. He knew the road ahead of me was going to be extremely difficult and that I would lose hope many times throughout the remainder of my life. He was aware that I would continue to make countless mistakes, be hurt by others, and at times, feel helpless.

The Lord was not only holding my hands while in the coma, He was with my parents every minute by reassuring them that He was in control of the situation. They were scared and in the middle of one of the most difficult times of their lives, yet they trusted God and remained hopeful He would heal me. They have told me since this experience has been over that they were motivated to keep the presence of everyone around me full of hope, energy, and optimism. They had a sign above my door which stated,

"Miracle in Progress" and also played contemporary Christian music in my room. It was important and necessary to them that every word that was spoken while in my room was positive and encouraging. They were unaware if I was capable of actually hearing them while I was in the coma but their belief was that if I was listening, then I needed to be lifted up with God's presence, not grief and sadness. I have also been informed that every time either my mom or fiancé walked into the room, my heart rate would noticeably increase which showed the physicians that I was somewhat cognizant of my surroundings.

As I opened my eyes after many weeks, evidently the first words I mouthed were, "I need a Diet Coke!" which does not surprise me, since most of my college career was spent drinking Diet Coke. At least He allowed me to keep my sense of humor.

He also gave me many more years to continue to grow and learn His ways. It has taken years for me to understand this but I am here to serve Him by serving others. I am honored to call myself a follower of Jesus Christ. I am not ashamed. I am a Christian.

He was privy to all of this while I was in the coma yet He spared my life. Thank you, Jesus. I am grateful for my life. I am blessed because you have allowed me to spend much more time with my family and friends and to continue to learn how to honor You. No matter the struggles I have already faced or future challenges, my life is a gift from You, Lord.

"One of the things I learned the hard way was that it doesn't pay to get discouraged. Keeping busy and making optimism a way of life can restore your faith in yourself."
Lucille Ball

"Mimi"

You asked the question, "How did you and mom handle it while I was in the coma?" I appreciate you giving me the opportunity to put pen to these thoughts and emotions. So, here goes...

When we got married, Mom and I knew what we wanted for our life as a family. Living through enough "rigged rodeos" or multiple challenges, we agreed on committing to His yoke, will and promises. God has afforded us many riches; including three wonderful children and six amazing grandchildren.

As you recall, you became sick the weekend of July 4th, 1994. You were admitted to the Intensive Care Unit of Sartori, which is our local hospital in Cedar Falls. Initially, they thought you might have Meningitis so they began running many tests. They ruled out Meningitis, but did recognize you had some sort of infection and that your kidneys were failing. We were constantly surrounded by family and friends; that coupled with our faith gave us strength. On the fourth day, our pastor, Homer Larsen, our loving family, and many of our friends gathered around your bed with us and Homer prayed. You opened your eyes for the first time in days! I don't think there was a dry eye in the room. Your mom and I left the room and were approached by two of your wonderful nurses who were brutally honest with us. Your condition had worsened and your doctor was recommending that you be air-flighted to Mayo Hospital in Rochester, Minnesota.

What a sight that was for us to watch our 23 year old, once healthy daughter, being taken by helicopter at 2:00 a.m. Again, God is so good! We were surrounded by caring nurses who gave hugs, well wishes, and offered prayer as the family scattered. We were blessed to have such a loving family. Uncle Jim and Aunt Mary immediately headed to Rochester to meet the helicopter. We wanted family there when you landed, even if you were not awake. Uncle Dick and Aunt Jean took Grandma with them to prepare for a trip to Rochester, Beth and your fiancé ran home and got clothes to join them, and your mom and I stayed back to see you off. We then went home and packed for a stay at Rochester.

When your mom and I arrived you were in the Intensive Care Unit. It was quite a sight we encountered as we stared through the two sets of doors. The sound of the ventilator, lights from the six blue boxes hooked up to you, plus many nurses working quietly and diligently painted a very solemn picture. Your mom and I just held each other and prayed. Dr. Meyer approached us later that day and gave us a report of what they knew and had done so far. They had induced a coma to relax you and save your strength. He said your heart needed to be monitored and that it did have some sort of infection. At that time, they diagnosed you with a staph infection plus multi-systems failure: your liver, kidneys, and lungs had shut down. They informed us you were very, very sick and they couldn't give any sort of prognosis. We clearly remember them reminding us that with ARDS-Adult Respitory Distress Syndrome (lung failure) there is a 10 day window. Those blue eyes of your mom's were staring at me looking for something to relieve the pain only a mother can hold. We already had faith, love, and commitment. Now we needed patience, trust in God and this incredible team of doctors. All I could do was hold her close, cry, and pray.

On the following day, the flight nurse came and just stood outside your room. I went out to thank him and he asked me to lunch to talk. He needed to tell someone what he had done to keep you alive during the flight. You really touched his heart honey and helped him to step up way beyond the call of duty. He had the bravery I needed and I told him so: going the extra mile for my daughter. What a hero! Only in America where the sanctity of life and a covenant with God is woven into our principles could a team of doctors like this exist. The ICU sustained the rigorous pace for 28 days.

"We asked for strength and God gave us dif-ficulties to make us strong.

We prayed for wisdom and God sent us prob-lems, the solving of them developed wisdom.

We pleaded for prosperity, and God gave us brain and brawn to WORK.

We pleaded for courage, and God gave us dangers to overcome.

We asked for power, and God gave us oppor-tunity.........and we had only been there 2 days." Author unknown

We wanted everything around you to be posi-tive and upbeat which actually helped us too. Your prognosis was bleak which caused much concern and fear. We decided to take all of our energies and put them into making your sur-

rounding as normal as possible. When entering your room, we would talk to you as if you were a part of the conversation. We discussed the weather, gave updates on friends and family, and watched your soap operas with you. The nurses combed your hair, gave baths and applied lotion; always talking and encouraging you. Friends and family came to visit and pray with us to show their love and support. Christian music could be heard coming from your room. We decorated your room, went through the hundreds of cards you received, AND PRAYED. We talked about how much had changed in such a short time. Weeks earlier you were graduating from UNI, looking for a teaching job, and planning a wedding. Your wedding dress was hanging in our kitchen; now, you were fighting for your life. At times it seemed so unbelievable. And yet, it was your life as it existed for now and so we continued to pray.

Mom was doing her best to keep all the family and friends harmonious but it was a stretch.

Sustaining our strength was fragmenting, so I grabbed mom, Michael, and Beth to pull it together. What we were doing wasn't going to work much longer, so from then on we needed to do this "Homer's Way."

This meant something huge to our family. We gathered as a family and I reminded them of something our pastor Homer used to preach frequently.

We all are precious and important to God. By his teaching our hearts over the years to strive to improve and trust in God's plan, we all knew once again we were precious and important. The peace, calm, and release were almost immediate. Your mom hugged me and whispered: "where did you come up with that?" I didn't have a clue.

Weeks later you successfully came out of the coma. Your first words were: "can I please have a diet coke?" Hilarious, right?

From there you were headed on your road to recovery. It was many months of physical, voca-

tional, and occupational therapy. At first, you couldn't even write your own name or follow a simple command. The rest of your recovery was full of great fortune along with great struggle, as it should be.

Honey, all of these things helped us to cope and get though a very difficult time. We were very blessed to have loving friends and family and a supportive church to get us through.

Your mom and I were talking many months later as to how we survived and got through all those weeks when we didn't know if you were going to live or die. She looked up at a cross stitch of "Footprints in the Sand" that Beth had made for us many years earlier and said. "I get it!" He carried us at the time we needed it most.

Honey,

When you know you're heading for a period of faith and reckoning please consider:

It might be well if we refrain from terms of winning versus defeat or even terms of obedience or disobedience in our journey to holiness. Instead, speak in terms of love, humility and gratitude to the Lord.

We love you,
Dad and Mom

I have always been a Packers fan!

My second year dancing at
Dixie's School of Dance, age 7.

I loved spending time at
Grandma and Grandpa's
during the summer.

I was invited to visit Governor Robert Ray while
I was Iowa's Poster Child for the American
Diabetes Association.

My Uncle Jim and I at a
Waldorf Junior College baseball game;
he was the coach.

My friend, David, and me before school.

My family spent a lot of summers on the boat in
Branson, Missouri.

This was taken before church on
Mother's Day in 1988.

I loved playing the trumpet in the
Cedar Falls High School Marching Band.
This was taken before a parade.

I became a member of the CFHS pom pon squad when I was a senior in high school.

The Alpha Delta Pi ladies at a formal.
Pictured from left to right are: Monica, Melissa,
Diane, Me, Heather, Sarah and Shelley.

Sarah posing on the
railroad tracks, age 6.

Sarah and I after one of her band
concerts when she was 10 years old.

This was Sarah's 11th birthday "hippy" party.
My brother, Michael, and his wife, Angie,
won the best-costume award.

Four generations of women: Me, Grandma Thelma, Mom and Sarah. I 'm so happy we took this picture since Grandma passed away less than one year later.

My family celebrating my nephew's (Landon) 3rd
birthday party. This was taken on January 14th, 2012.

Chapter 13

(1994-1995)
Self-Forgiveness

≈≈≈≈≈

Daniel 9:9

*"The Lord our God is merciful
and forgiving, even though we have
rebelled against him;"*

(NIV)

My growth in faith has been constant throughout my life. It has had many peaks and valleys during the journey. I have never doubted His existence, but I have questioned Him far too many times and demanded reasons for things which have happened to me or to those I love. So many times in my life, I have been certain that I am wiser than God and that my plans are better than His.

The first major example of this was when I heard the doctors say the following words to me, "Ami, we are not sure if you'll ever be able to walk again. We've never had a patient make it this far after what you're body has gone through. Therefore, we do not know what to expect with your healing or even your future. There is no actual sever in your spine. The abscess in your spinal column which was caused by the infection, may eventually heal itself, but we are unsure. We are going to remain cautiously optimistic."

It had been determined by the doctors that the staph infection had depleted the oxygen in my spine which resulted in the abscess. The area in my spine which was lacking oxygen was now of no use and basically dead. When I first awoke, I was not able to move my legs and had limited use of my arms and hands. By the grace of God, the function in my upper body returned and that has been something that I have had to learn to be grateful for. I mentioned earlier about the times when I chose to neglect my diabetes by skipping insulin injections. The doctors never came right out and said this to me but my personal belief is that my poor health status was a major factor of how I got the staph infection. How, you ask?

When I was in college, I did most things that typical college students do. I stayed up late hours, either studying or hanging out with friends. I went to entirely too many parties and consumed alcohol in excess at times and did not eat the healthiest foods. This can be somewhat manageable for the college student who has no major health issues but for a young woman who has had an auto-immune (diabetes) disease for 17-18 years, it can prove to be harmful, life-altering or deadly. When I was finally awake enough to comprehend what had happened to me and that I had somehow contracted a staph infection, I knew in my heart that my lack of diabetic control had played a major role in my illness. My immune system was not strong enough to fight it off and my body had to basically go into sleep mode in order to survive the trauma to my system. I am sure you can imagine my hope in returning to *normal* being able to walk again.

"Cautiously optimistic" were the words that initially gave me the false hope to walk again. I now admit that I was in a form of the big word DENIAL! In my mind, the only word I really heard was optimistic. I was unable to accept it. God would not demand this from me, would He and if He was, then why?

My inability to accept my new reality lasted during my months at rehab. I believed that I knew more than God did regarding my situation. He certainly was not serious about this. I was a good person who loved the Lord. I had never done anything too terrible. Of course, I was a sinner and had made countless mistakes in my life, but this was a permanent, cruel punishment from God.

"Why me, Lord?"

I repeated those words out loud and in my private prayers continuously for the first year or two after 1994. There was absolutely no redeeming reason why this was happening to me. I had just graduated from college and had two unofficial job offers. We had recently gotten engaged and had the entire wedding planned.

I did not know it at the time but my parents evidently had my cap and gown, my wedding dress, and a hospital robe hanging in their kitchen side by side for weeks following my Mayo stay.

On the first hanger was the tangible accomplishment of the years of hard work receiving my degree. They had been with me emotionally and somewhat physically during my years at UNI. They knew what it meant to me to have that diploma. I was the first grandchild to have a college education and to walk across a stage to hear the words, "Ladies and gentlemen, the University of Northern Iowa graduating class of 1994." For me it was not just my reward but a symbol of the sacrifices my family ahead of me had made.

The next hanger in the doorway of my parents' kitchen held my long, beaded wedding dress, which had yet to be worn by me. This represented my future to all who had previously seen it. Every time I had looked at my dress, I envisioned my fiancé and myself in our little home with all of our new items given to us at our wedding. I saw us both teaching at an elementary school and eating dinner together after a long day of "changing the world!"

Of course, I saw our future children too. Our imaginary daughter's name would be Jordan Leigh and our son's name would be Bradley Dean (Dean is my dad's middle name). Our entire life was in front of us.

On the third hanger hung a hospital gown I had worn at Mayo. This must have been quite a reality shock for my parents every time they glanced at the visible reminder of what had recently happened. Yet they remained hopeful, persistent, and committed to me.

My dad spent his days with me in the rehabilitation unit. He was my saving grace and my literal protector because he knew how physically and emotionally exhausted I was. He was keenly aware of the fact that my body was not yet ready to learn all of the new ways to survive. I do not remember many specifics about my tenure in the hospital but I do know that I did not feel understood nor respected by some of the professionals who worked there.

There was one particular care giver who said the following words to me, which left me feeling worthless, "You should feel blessed you can still move your arms, Ami. There are many people here who aren't as lucky as you."

Please understand that I am seventeen years into my paralysis, I totally agree with that statement. The Lord has continued to provide me with the strength to persevere and be grateful. However, when I was twenty-three years old and was just learning how to cope with my loss, those were the last words I needed to hear. Not forgetting to mention that the care provider who gave me that particular feedback scurried out of my hospital room with their working body, leaving me in my bed unable to move my legs. I would lie there doubting myself, God, and those around me. Then I would get so angry! If it had been a person with a disability, then I could have understood them better. Although I would not have appreciated their words at the time, I would have respected them because I would have known that they had lived it.

The Lord had always allowed me to stay optimistic and hopeful. I recall all of the previous health scares I had been able to avert or navigate around. The fact that He had allowed me to accomplish as many things in my life in spite of being diabetic for years, led me to believe that I had be able to "dodge another bullet". I just knew that this would pass and that I would soon be upright and able to be myself. I was the young woman who just three months earlier had been running errands to plan her wedding, finishing up student teaching, and driving to job interviews. Where was she? I would lie in my hospital bed pouring my heart out to God.

"Lord, please heal my body completely. Make me the person I just was three months ago. Let me be able to feel my entire body. Please, Jesus, I'm begging you to let me walk and especially dance again. I cannot fathom not ever being able to do normal things again. I'm so jealous of my brother, sister, and everybody! And, God, I certainly don't want to live the rest of the life being resentful and bitter. And, watching others being able to do those things in front of me makes me mourn for who I was and need to be again. Who am I, Lord?" I will never know why God allowed me to experience the summer and fall of 1994 but after many years of not being able to forgive myself, I have finally accepted that He forgave me long ago. I no longer carry that burden in my heart. In fact, I have realized that His plan for my life has always included that summer. For the record: lesson learned!

"The only thing we can do is play on the one thing we have, and that is our attitude - I am convinced that life is 10% what happens to me and 90% how I react to it."
Charles Swindoll

Friends from the Heart Benefit
(1994)

After three months in the physical rehabilitation unit in the hospital, I was honored to have two friends from UNI organize a benefit for me. Lisa David, a good friend from another Sorority on campus (Alpha Phi) and Stacy Farmer, from my Sorority, did an amazing job with implementing an event that brought hundreds of my friends and people from my community together to raise money for the expenses that were related to my disability. The local television station (KWWL) was there to catch the highlights as well as entertainment, music, and delicious food. Because of the monies that were raised by the caring people who attended, I was able to purchase a new handicapped accessible van, so I could regain a lot of my independence.

In fact, I have been driving ever since and cannot imagine not being able to go have the freedoms I have.

Thanks to the individuals from the Waterloo and Cedar Falls Communities for making this possible!

This song was written by my friend, Enrique Ochoa, who was one of my youth counselors during my high school years. He sang this at the Friends From The Heart Benefit. I have loved this song since I heard it!

"Ami's Song"

Oh, the memories of you

They are plenty and few

Are the moments we've not seen you smile.

Though this moment is hard,

Our love is not far

As you lie there in bed for awhile.

Ami, we know that you hear

And we know that He hears

The prayers we give up for you.

Ami, we know that you listen,

Please know we are missing you.

So many lives you have touched

It's a joy to see so much

Of how you are cared for and loved.

All of our days are lived under God's gaze,

In the darkest of night, there is hope.

Ami, you know we are here

And you know He is here

Watching and caring for you.

Ami, we know you listen,

Please know we are missing you.

Today,

A thankful surprise!

Today,

You opened your eyes!

Ami, we know that you heard

And we know that He heard

The prayers we gave up for you.

Ami, we know you listened

you know we were missing you.

It's so good to talk now to you.

Enrique Ochoa—1994

Chapter 14

(1994-1999)
Blessings from Above

━━━〰〰〰〰━━━

John 14:1

"Do not let your hearts be troubled. Trust in God; trust also in me."

(NIV)

O nce I had finally learned how to cope and live my life from a seated position, my fiancé and I were able to formally start our life together. He had been offered a job in a town less than one hour away and we were able to have a beautiful wedding ceremony. I finally got to wear my dress! It was 1998 and he had gotten to be very close to my family and I felt the same about his. My brother, sister, fiancé, and I would often spend time together. We enjoyed eating home-made nachos, watching movies (although I was still very fatigued and would fall asleep during the movies and need to be told how they ended) and laughing about crazy things! It seemed as if our life was gaining a sense of normalcy and, in spite of an occasional sad moment where I mourned for my pre-disability self, we seemed happy.

We were aware of the fact that my kidneys had failed during the coma, but they had somehow gained a lot of their function back. It was enough to return to a typical schedule but we were acutely cognizant that they would not last forever and this proved to come to fruition in 1999. I started to become increasingly tired again so I went in for blood tests and was told by my dear nephrologist that I would more than likely need dialysis and/or a transplant within the next year. Since my husband was at work and unable to take the day off, my dad drove me to the appointment and back to our home that evening. Dad stayed at our house until it looked as if I was emotionally stable enough for him to return home. My husband and I spent the remainder of the evening discussing our options for the future.

That evening, I had an extremely vivid dream that still remains fresh in my mind over 12 years later. My husband and I were in an elevator and it suddenly started to descend rapidly and was destined to crash. In my dream, I yelled out the words, "Lord, please take us into your kingdom!" At that point, I woke up in tears reaching for my husband next to me in our bed. I believe that I instinctively knew that He was going to provide healing for me and although I was very scared for my survival, my subconscious knew that I was protected. He afforded me that security and peace by giving my mom the courage and strength to agree to be tested to be my kidney donor and wouldn't you know—she was a 50% marker match which meant that she was a viable donor for me. She and I underwent pre-surgical testing at the University of Iowa and had our surgery on November 11, 1999. Not many mothers can say that they gave their child life twice in one lifetime, but my mom can!

After we recuperated from our surgery, Mom returned to work at John Deere and I was given a new lease on life. I was once again full of energy, had an appetite, and was motived to live my life to the fullest. I have often wondered why I have been given so many miracles and been privileged to know so many loving, caring people in my short life. I do not think I will ever know why all of the seemingly hard times I have gone through have ended up becoming blessings but I try to stay focused on the fact that He will finish what He has started in my life, a chance to be the best person I can be and give Him all of the glory.

"You can do it if you think you can!"
Napoleon Hill

Chapter 15

(2001)
The Love of my Life

⟞⟪⟫⟞

Psalms 103:17

"But from everlasting to everlasting the LORD's love is with those who fear him, and his righteousness with their children's children."

(NIV)

I have always dreamed of having children like most young girls do. Christmastime usually included countless hours of preparing and organizing wish-lists of "babies," blankets, bottles, and other essentials.

When I got older, I imagined with vivid detail how I would tell my future husband that we were expecting a baby. I told myself that it would more than likely be a romantic dinner with the decedent dessert being garnished with a rattle or a bulletin board announcement in our neighborhood.

However, by the time I was in high school, I became honest within myself and admitted that if I was going to be a mom, then whoever my husband was going to be would have to agree to adopt a child. Although I was not yet ready to openly admit to others that I had not taken very good care of body, I told myself that it would not be wise to ever carry a child in my womb. By no means did this ever sway my desire to be called "mommy." I am not sure why it is that most females are born with nurturing attributes but it certainly seems that God's plan for procreation includes this.

In 2000, I started reminding my husband of my desire to be a mommy and mentioned many times the importance of family. We had been living in the same home for four years and were established in our neighborhood. He also had a secure teaching job in our small town. I started doing research online and via the telephone while he was at work and discovered different opportunities for adopting. He would come home from school and I would literally almost jump out of my wheelchair with excitement after reading about these children!

It did not take us long to find the perfect match for us. She was a little girl with blonde hair and bright brown eyes. She was eighteen months old and obviously the cutest little lady I had ever laid my eyes upon. Her chubby cheeks had so much life in them and I loved everything about her.

From the first second I laid my eyes on her, I knew in my heart that God had made us to be mother and daughter.

She was standing in the room of the adoption office looking out the window. There was a young woman holding her miniature body high enough to see outside. On her little body, she wore a pale yellow dress which emphasized the depth of her deep, dark eyes.

We slowly strolled into the room and just observed her for a few minutes. She was extremely curious about what was happening outside the window. With the young woman's prompting, she would point to the moving cars and at the people coming and going. Oh, I just wanted to go over and pick her up! I loved her from the moment I saw her.

I have known of other people who have adopted and although they grow to love their children "as if they were their own" it can take an adjustment period to feel that powerful feeling. I am not sure why, but God blessed me with immediate love and affection for this little girl. He is awesome and I thank Him every day for this gift.

It took a couple more months to officially become a family. What a beautiful addition to us and a perfect little human being! I now felt right saying the word family. What was even better was calling Sarah my daughter. But the sweetest word I had heard at that point in my life was when she first called me "Mommy." I had never felt such pride for who I was as a woman until she and I would be seen together in public.

Once we got her home, she quickly learned how to carefully climb up in my lap and ride with me in the chair. Eventually as she became more independent (age 2), we would run all of our errands together. Sarah walked beside my wheelchair holding onto the armrest. Somehow, she almost instinctively knew to stay beside me and never let go of my chair. We obviously never went to places that were crowded or very noisy but we would go out to such places as the grocery store and our shopping mall in the middle of the day.

She and I spent our days as most moms and young children: doing craft activities, Play doh, watching movies, and of course, trying to get her to actually take a nap! To this day, I laugh out loud when I recall the times when I would turn on her soft music, close her window shades, and rub her back to encourage her to close her eyes for rest time. I laugh because what often happened was I would fall asleep while leaning over her tiny little toddler bed as I was rubbing her back. The funniest part of this memory is that when I would open my eyes when the CD was over, Sarah would be leaning over me playing with my hair! Needless to say, Sarah was rarely a child who would actually take a nap. She loved to always be "in-the-mix" and I think she just did not want to miss out on anything.

We would also enjoy going on walks across our small town to get to Dairy Queen for an ice cream cone. The DQ was probably at least one mile away, so of course her little legs would become fatigued during the stroll. About ¾ of the way to the Dairy Queen, Sarah would ask to climb on my lab in my wheelchair. She and I would continue our way for our ice cream cones. We always made it work out for the best.

Sarah and I also spent years when she was younger driving an hour away to her dance class where she took tap and eventually gymnastics. She always did an amazing job at her recitals and, of course, she knew her dances very well. I was always so proud of her when she was on stage! The trips to her classes and back home were wonderful bonding opportunities for us as we would sing songs all the way to and from class and play games such as *I Spy* or an improvised version of *Hang Man*.

There were many times when she was in kindergarten and she only had school on Monday, Wednesday, and Friday that we would leave for dance class early enough to spend a few hours with my parents and my grandma since they all lived in the same city as her class. Tuesday afternoons were usually deemed "Gammy, Papa, and Great Grandma days." I hope now, years later, that Sarah enjoyed those days as much as I did.

Sarah is and will remain the biggest blessing the Lord has ever given to me. I am grateful to her biological parents for loving Sarah enough to give her the life she has had with my family. I am honored and humbled to call myself her mom and feel a great responsibility in raising her up to be a believer in Jesus. As she and I have matured in our years, I have acknowledged to God and myself that children are a gift given only by Him. Unfortunately, it seems as though certain people in this world treat them more as a possession.

We, as parents, cannot manage nor control every aspect of our children's lives, but we are called by God to treat them with love, kindness, and respect. If we do not set that example, then how will they learn any other way?

*"Children are the living messages
we send to a time we will not see."
John W. Whitehead, founder
Rutherford Institute*

"Find your Wings"

It's only for a moment you are mine to hold

The plans that heaven has for you

Will all too soon unfold

So many different prayers I'll pray

For all that you might do

But most of all I'll want to know

You're walking in the truth

And if I never told you

I want you to know

As I watch you grow

I pray that God would fill your heart with dreams

And that faith gives you the courage

To dare to do great things

I'm here for you whatever this life brings

So let my love give you roots

And help you find your wings

May passion be the wind

That leads you through your days

And may conviction keep you strong

Guide you on your way

May there be many moments

That make your life so sweet

Oh, but more than memories

It's not living if you don't reach for the sky

I'll have tears as you take off

But I'll cheer as you fly

Mark Harris

The Line Between The Two—2005

Chapter 16

Monica: My Inspiration

~~~~~~~~

1 Corinthians 8:3
"But whoever loves God
is known by God."
(NIV)

Monica Williams Shannon was a friend of mine during my years at the University of Northern Iowa. She and I were Alpha Delta Pi Sisters and spent many hours together experiencing college life. Monica was extremely outspoken and did not even try to hide her true feelings or beliefs about life. She was sometimes perceived as rude by those who did not appreciate her soft heart underneath her occasional tough exterior.

Although Monica and I had many good times together during school, I would not have considered her to be a close friend until after graduation. About one year before I became ill with my staph infection, Monica started experiencing tremendous migraine headaches and unpredictable mood swings. We were still active members of our sorority and extremely busy getting ready to graduate when she was diagnosed with a brain tumor. Unfortunately, I do not have many vivid memories of college the year prior to my illness, so I cannot accurately portray what Monica was going through at that time. However, I can tell you how instrumental Monica was to my healing and faith walk during my tenure at rehab and the following years.

While I was in the rehabilitation unit, Monica would often come visit me and offer words of encouragement. What I have not shared is that she was undergoing chemotherapy at the time. I remember her spending many hours with me in my hospital room sitting beside my hospital bed, speaking kind, supportive words to me. She and I discussed how we both felt alone and isolated from our friends and the "normal" world. We cried together and tried to cheer each other up in spite of her balding head and my useless body (that is how I saw myself at the time).

Monica survived the first few years with brain cancer. She met a wonderful, supportive man Don Shannon. They married and had a daughter named Sydney. Moni was an underlying reminder of what the human spirit can accomplish. She and I emailed throughout the years, but did not stay in touch as much as we both wished until I received a call from a mutual sorority friend (Molly Cormaney). Molly informed me that Monica's health had taken a turn for the worst.

Monica and I were able to once again nurture our friendship during the last year of her short life. In those last months, I was blessed to learn that she was a follower of Jesus Christ and had a very strong faith. She confided in me during telephone conversations admitting that she was hesitant to speak with anyone outside her family in fear of "not sounding normal." She was acutely aware that the tumor in her brain was growing stronger and, unfortunately, controlling her thought process and speech patterns. But she had her hilarious wit and humor until the end when she laughed about her two year old daughter, Sydney, trying to "manipulate the babysitter" or put things in the toilet that "just don't belong."

When Molly and I attended her funeral together, Monica's mom pulled me aside and expressed that Monica considered me to be an inspiration to her. I was humbled, mostly because she was and continues to be my inspiration. One of Alpha Delta Pi's promises we make to each other is loyalty. I will continue to be loyal to Monica by honoring her memory. I know that one day, she and I will reunite in heaven. You will know it is us, because we will be singing Alpha Delta Pi Rush/Recruitment songs together! Not very well, I must add!

"A friend should be one in whose understanding
and virtue we can equally confide,
and whose opinion we can value at once for its
justness and its sincerity."
Robert Hall

Chapter 17

(2007)

The End of Life as We Know It

~~~~~~~~~~

Philippians 4:19

"And my God will meet all your needs

according to the riches of his

glory in Christ Jesus."

(NIV)

In 2007, my husband was offered an amazing career opportunity in the Des Moines Area which was promising. We had been so excited to get out of our small community that I now believe that I started to "over-do it" the few months prior to moving.

For my husband, it was obvious. A new career adventure where he could finally do exactly what he wanted.

Sarah did not understand what an opportunity this was for her because she was only seven years old. I saw it as a way for her to meet more friends and experience much more. Sarah met a great friend Abbie who is still one of her best friends. I hope they will continue to communicate for years to come.

I envisioned only great things for my family once we got to the Des Moines Area. The obvious benefits for my husband and Sarah, and for me, were accessibility! I was looking forward to being able to frequent more places besides Pamida (although Pamida is a wonderful store for smaller towns). I craved something larger than that and the grocery store. These two stores were both newer and wheelchair accessible. Anywhere else I went was usually a challenge for me. Even getting into Sarah's elementary school was a struggle. It was an older building with three flights of stairs connected by a lift which took 5-7 minutes to climb and of course, Sarah's classroom was on the third floor!

During the years we had lived there, we met some very kind people including our next door neighbors and friends that worked with my husband. I cannot explain (because even I do not know) what was missing from my life during that time but something definitely was.

In my past, I had always been included in activities which was a great way to meet people, but this environment did not seem to offer anything that piqued my interests. I found myself to be extremely lonely and to be perfectly honest I was bored. My husband and I had agreed that I would be a stay-at-home mom and I believed that Sarah deserved to be in a home where her mom could be an active part of her life. My husband's career provided us with the opportunity for me to stay with Sarah and I believe it was one of the wisest decisions we ever made for our family.

We chose to build a new home in the Des Moines Area since I was in need of an accessible house. I had been blessed enough to receive monies for home modifications many years prior and we had quite a bit of equity to put into new construction. Anyone who has ever built a new home knows that it is a stressful time because there are many decisions to make and agree upon and months to wait for the home to be completed. Because of the fact that we had to wait almost one year before we could move in and there were few accessible options for temporary housing, we lived in a tiny duplex approximately 30 minutes away from my husband's new job.

That year was the start of hard times (as I see it) for my family. Sarah was now in 2nd grade so I was comfortable going back to work on a full-time basis and got hired at the Junior High in the same district as Sarah and my husband. Halfway into the school year, I started feeling ill and fatigued. Between working 35 hours a week, building our home, and going back to school (I had begun taking Special Education classes to receive my Master's Degree), I was so tired that I had a difficult time keeping my eyes open. I sensed that my health was failing and that my husband was unhappy but I could not put my finger on the cause of our arguments.

I then chose to resign from my job so I could have more energy for our family and focus on my well-being and health. My husband and I spoke and agreed to hire a part-time care-giver to help me during the daytime with things that I needed and with household duties so our evenings could be spent together as a family. But this did not help. I found myself feeling worse and very concerned about my kidney function and our family's future. I was not aware at the time, but the stress I was feeling was causing increased health issues and would only worsen in the next three years.

"He knows not his own strength that hath not met adversity."

Ben Jonson

The Serenity Prayer

God grant me the serenity
to accept the things I cannot change;
courage to change the things I can;
and wisdom to know the difference.

Living one day at a time;
Enjoying one moment at a time;
Accepting hardships as the pathway to peace;
Taking, as He did, this sinful world
as it is, not as I would have it;
Trusting that He will make all things right
if I surrender to His Will;
That I may be reasonably happy in this life
and supremely happy with Him
Forever in the next.
Amen.

—*Reinhold Niebuhr*

Chapter 18

(2008-2010)
Will I Ever Feel Loved Again?

—〰〰〰—

Philippians 4:13
*"I can do all things through him
who gives me strength."*
(NIV)

W e finally were able to move into our lovely, new (accessible) home when Sarah was in 3rd grade. Our family was enjoying our new surroundings and meeting more people to enjoy our spare time. Yet I felt as if we were both unfulfilled in our marriage and my heart and mind could feel my husband pulling away emotionally and physically. It is hard to fathom this now, but two more years passed before I was acutely aware that our future was in jeopardy.

As I try to honestly look back at those years, what I believe happened was that neither one of us felt as if we mattered to one another and we basically just continued to go through the motions of being a married couple. I can only speak for myself, but I know that I was beginning to question his love and devotion to me and our marriage. The most important person who should have been in the center of our marriage was not present because we neglected to let *Him* in.

Although I have felt like Christ has been next to me for my entire life, I made a major mistake by allowing myself to lose focus from Him and get distracted from His power and love. I know within my heart that this is the reason my mind was overwhelmed with so many burdens. Because of those underlying worries and fears, my health continued to worsen until I was directed by my doctor to be admitted into the local hospital for testing. The tests revealed that my kidney function was extremely inadequate and that my life was again in the balance.

I was so scared for my family; especially for Sarah. I spent one week in that hospital and most days and evenings, I was alone. I wondered what God was asking me to do with this news and had nobody (except two friends) to share my fears. It was somewhat reminiscent of my days when I was a young girl and would spend countless days in hospitals except now there did not seem to be a valid reason why I was alone. We only lived fifteen minutes away from the hospital.

I was discharged from the hospital on a Saturday with many fears in my heart. I prayed that God would restore my kidney function and that our marriage would strengthen and be filled with love. My desire for all good and honest things in this lifetime are not only for myself but for Sarah to have a childhood where she is surrounded by people who are filled with the Holy Spirit, honorable integrity, and security.

By His grace (again!), I was blessed with the news that my kidney had regained some function and that was enough good news for me to feel confident that I could go home. As the discharge nurse was giving me my instructions before I left, she mentioned that I had a very small red mark on my fanny. I had never had a mark on my bottom before (after being in my wheelchair for almost sixteen years) and did not realize the possibilities of a negative outcome at the time. I was thrilled to get home to see Sarah and went home to be reunited.

In the following months, our marriage was no better than it had been before I was hospitalized. I begged my husband to see a counselor with me for couple's therapy. I called our pastor and he suggested a woman who was a member of our congregation and she agreed to see us separately and together. We met with her for a few months yet it seemed to just give my husband an avenue to openly express his dissatisfaction and apparent frustration with me, the disability, and the fact that he was "required" to care for me at times. Those sessions were full of tears, worries, and frustrations. I kept asking myself what had happened to us and how we were ever going to get through it all without scarring Sarah emotionally.

Things got increasingly difficult once we discovered that the little red mark on my fanny had turned into a full-blown open wound. Things rapidly took a turn for the worse. The pinnacle of grief for me at that time was the day that our therapist called me into her office unexpectedly so that my husband could tell me that he was considering filing for divorce. I was understandably concerned beyond belief and cried for days after. How would I ever financially provide for Sarah? Where would I live? I knew from what he had said that he desired to keep our accessible home. Was I going to have to start my life all over again? How would my health ever improve with all of the stresses that were upon me? How would I ever trust any man again with my feelings and future? The questions kept flooding my mind.

For some reason, he did not file the papers for a few more weeks. There were even times when I believed that we would be able to find the love that we needed to repair our marriage. As I look back, I now see that there were other factors that came into play which slowed the process. In the meantime, I continued to see our therapist by myself to try to navigate through the pending physical and emotional changes. She was extremely helpful in providing Christ-centered advice on how to get through the pain, fear, and stress. With much prayer and consideration, I took the advice of our therapist and my doctors and decided to temporarily go to my parents' home two hours away to physically and emotionally heal. At that time, my doctors were telling me that it could take up to six weeks to heal from my wound. I was also informed that I would probably be able to undergo a plastic surgery on my bottom in order to speed up the healing. My parents, therapist, health care team, and I separately discussed what would be the best case scenario for complete healing and it was agreed by all to pursue seeing a plastic surgeon for an assessment.

My decision to go with my parents to see a surgeon was not as promising as we had expected because we were told that my fanny was not nearly healthy enough to be operated on. We drove back to their home to discuss how we were going to handle the news. We knew that my husband and Sarah were back in the Des Moines Area and that my marriage and the future of our family were at stake. The decision regarding how long to stay with my parents' was decided for me when I received a text message, followed by a packet in the mail by my husband's attorney. He had finally decided to file for the divorce. Once again the tears began to flow because I realized that I would never adequately heal without proper healthcare in my parents' community. The tears became more intense when I had to eventually face that the absolute most heart-wrenching time of my life would be missing my child.

"Healing does not mean going back to the way things were before, but rather allowing what is now to move us closer to God."

Ram Dass

Chapter 19

(2010)
Who Determines My Worth?

⚊⚊⚋⚌⚋⚌⚋⚊⚊

John 16:33

*"I have told you these things, so that
in me you may have peace.
In this world you will have trouble. But
take heart! I have overcome the world."*

(NIV)

I have prayed for almost a year asking the Lord to guide my decision about including this chapter in my memoir. After much prayer and reflection, I have decided to include certain scenarios that contribute to who I am in Christ. I do not mention these things to hurt anyone nor depict anyone unfairly. I do this because it helps us all understand how Jesus can conquer all of our fears, insecurities, and lies that Satan puts in our lives. There are many situations I have chosen to exclude from this entire memoir because they are just too painful to mention.

I am hoping it is normal to feel unloved when a marriage is about to end, wondering if anyone will ever want you again. I had begun to believe that I was unworthy of anyone but my husband because I was disabled. After years of feeling that I was no longer desirable or intelligent, I now believe that my lack of confidence probably showed on the outside to others.

I knew what my family and friends were telling me. I was a kind, loving, occasionally funny and interesting person to know. However, the fact that I was in need of physical assistance on a daily basis from my husband and that he did not seem to believe that I had adjusted to my disability were underlying burdens and left me with a heart laden with guilt. I often asked myself, "Was he right about me, because we had been together so long and he knew my fears and insecurities?"

Beginning in the year of 2007, I'd had a few moments when I really struggled with what my purpose was and who I was destined to become. Once my husband and I started having troubles, I lost even more of my self-worth, pride in who I was, and admittedly, there were moments when I questioned if it was necessary for me to be alive. I had gotten to the point where I felt so tired and sickly that I believed that those who loved me would be better off without me.

"Who had I become? Was it even worthwhile for me to be here?"

Those were fleeting moments, because I quickly realized the hurt Sarah and my loved ones would feel if I didn't continue to fight my doubts of who I was, and I eventually accepted that I just needed to find a way to once again love myself and be the best person I could be— in spite of my physical situation.

(those of you who have experienced divorce probably realize that that is not a good time to try to raise your self-esteem) Besides, I knew that it wasn't in me to actually take my own life; I would never purposely inflict that never-ending grief on those I'd leave behind.

As I look back at those lonely times, I know that I wasn't allowing God to guide me through my sadness. I was choosing to give the enemy my mind, which could've been my physical and emotional demise. I just wasn't sure how to pull myself up. That was frustrating, since I'd thought that I was typically capable of finding solutions to my problems. I had been a "go-getter" my entire life and the new feeling of not knowing how to help myself was different for me. I was at an emotional stand still and knew I had to figure something out, so I started begging God to show me the way.

The thing that complicated the situation was that my physical health was so unstable I felt like I had no extra stores of energy to draw from for motivation and strength. So, when I did feel like God was directly motivating me; through a Christian song on the radio, a fleeting moment of inspiration, or even a kind word from someone, my physical and emotional fatigue would override the desires within my heart-everything except my love and desire to be there for Sarah, emotionally and physically.

Being without Sarah was absolutely unbearable and I pray that I will never go through anything as painful as that again in my life. I missed my sweet, loving daughter so much. I yearned just to hear her voice and touch her sweet face. Tears welled up in my eyes when I imagined tucking her in her bed at night or even something as small as greeting her when she came in the door after school. My heart felt broken as I missed out on the "little things." I needed her as much as she needed me and I feared I would never get the opportunity to experience being her mom again. It was, by far, the hardest and what seemed to be the longest time in my life.

Prayers and continual reminders of His love for Sarah and me always allowed some temporary relief, but the day-to-day reminder that she and I were not together was unbearable most of the time.

I cried non-stop and just couldn't navigate myself out of the pain. I knew that I'd lost the my husband, home, community, friends, and I even grieved the loss of our dog, but being without Sarah literally felt as if I'd lost the ability to breathe.

I kept telling myself that "you're the adult here; stop crying and get yourself out of this!" But, I continued to question my worth at that point and the old tapes of self-doubt would play in my head. I would ask myself the following questions:

"Ami, what have you really accomplished in this life? Yes, you have a college degree, but you haven't even been a 'real' teacher. You're no longer pretty. No man even ever looks at you because you're in a stupid wheelchair. And now you're so sickly that you're not even fun to be around."

But then I would recall all of the people in my life, my family and true, Christian friends, who now I know always loved me unconditionally for who I am and haven't lost on the inside. These particular folks do not just "blow smoke" to make me feel better about myself. They're honest, yet loving and gentle at the same time. I struggled with that internal conflict of not knowing if I was worthy of love and verbal affection for many years and it eventually took a toll on my mind, spirit, and body.

I recognize now that my insecurities weren't invented in my head. I take that back; when I initially got in the chair I obviously wondered who I was and what I was going to do with the rest of my life from a sitting position. I truly believe that's a normal part of the grieving process. But, the things I had been experiencing had often led me to believe that I would no longer be successful-in life or love.

Whenever these doubts would enter my head, I felt as if I was not receiving the encouragement I needed to overcome them. Towards the end of our relationship there were times when I questioned if I had ever been loved during our marriage. And, yet, I held out hope that I would be capable of saying the right words to help him gain the desire to stay in our marriage. I told myself that Sarah deserved parents who could stick together, even though they were unhappy. I still don't know (nor ever will know) what would have been the best for her in that situation. Only God knows.

During those years, I allowed myself to lose who my parents had raised me to be: confident, strong, and positive. My heart (which I now know was God telling me) kept saying that I was still a good person who deserved love and affection. Still, the detrimental effects on me were overwhelming!

This internal struggle still exists inside of me. I pray continuously that my heart and God's grace will help me overcome this fight within myself. Satan has a sneaky way of making us doubt ourselves, our loved ones, and eventually, God. I believe that just as He puts certain people in our lives when we need them the most, Satan tries to sabotage God's plan by planting evil around us when we are at our weakest. Remember, he has studied the Bible inside and out. He is crafty and manipulative and will do anything to make us angry at our Creator. Fortunately, God's will and plan for our prosperity are stronger than the enemy's.

"You would not have the wisdom and knowledge you now possess were it not for the setbacks you have faced, the mistakes you have made and the suffering you have endured."
Robin Sharma, Who Will Cry When You Die?

"He Will Carry Me"

I call, You hear me
I've lost it all
And it's more then I can bear
I feel so empty

You're strong, I'm weary
I'm holding on
But I feel like giving in
But still You're with me

And even though I'm walking
Through the valley of the shadow
I will hold tight to the hand of Him
Whose love will comfort me
And when all hope is gone
And I've been wounded in the battle
He is all the strength that I will ever need
He will carry me

I know I'm broken

But You alone

Can mend this heart of mine

You're always with me

And even though I'm walking

Through the valley of the shadow

I will hold tight to the hand of Him

Whose love will comfort me

And when all hope is gone

And I've been wounded in the battle

He is all the strength that I will ever need

He will carry me He Will Carry Me

And even though I feel so lonely

Like I have never been before

You never said it would be easy

But You said You'd see me through the storm

And even though I'm walking

Through the valley of the shadow

I will hold tight to the hand of Him

Whose love will comfort me

And when all hope is gone

And I've wounded in the battle

He is all the strength that I will ever need

He will carry me, He Carry Me, He Will Me

Mark Schultz

The Best of Mark Schultz—2011

Chapter 20

(2010-2011)
Perseverance is the Only Choice for Me

—⟞〰〰〰⟝—

James 1:4

"Perseverance must finish its work so that you may be mature and complete, not lacking anything."

(NIV)

I will never understand why tragedy and seemingly unnecessary things occur. God's design is certainly bigger than ours and it is true that He has the big picture. If He created us and knew the number of hairs on our head before we were even born, then how could it be any different?

When we are challenged to change our ways or endure hard times, a lot of us question Him. How many times have you questioned God about our suffering? Or the infamous question we have all asked, "Why me?"

Because of the continual worsening of the wound on my fanny, I was told by my doctors to literally stay off my bottom and lay on my side in bed to relieve the pressure and I had to do that for over one and a half years! I was able to be out of bed for no more than two hours a day. It was a very lonely time in my life. Although my siblings and their families, friends, and my parents tried desperately to keep me company, watching them come-and-go from the house was torture. In fact, a majority of this memoir was written on my iPad while I lay on my side. I could not do much else with that time but write down my thoughts, cry, and mourn for my loss. How could I even say the word "perseverance" when I could not imagine even having a future ahead of me? If I was going to live, then what kind of a life was it going to be?

I felt like the cards were stacked against me. My health had failed to the point where I had lost my marriage. My "friends," whom I cared for and thought cared for me were believing things about me that were certainly not accurate. They were believing that I had chosen to be absent from Sarah's life.

My hospital stays seemed non-stop locally and to Saint Mary's Hospital in Rochester, Minnesota. There were probably close to ten times when I was either in the emergency room or lying in my hospital room as an inpatient while talking to Sarah, my attorney, or my soon to be ex-husband, without any of them even knowing. The last thing I wanted was for them to know everything that was happening to me and my body.

First and foremost, I did not want Sarah to worry about me. I knew her world was already filled with worry, anxiety, and confusion. My husband, and ironically, people who should have focused on keeping our child with both parents equally (although in two separate homes) questioned my ability to be a mom. Unfortunately, because of my disability and health concerns, I had evidently become "unable to care for her."

As I now reflect, I believe the only thing a lot of them saw was the wheelchair, not the woman and mother who was sitting in it. This could obviously lead me into another avenue of expression, but I am not allowing myself to even go there!

Regardless of what they presumed the facts were, I had always been Sarah's primary source of emotional strength and also been a stay-at-home mom constantly involved in her life. I was told that because I may need another kidney transplant before Sarah turned eighteen, it was not wise for her to live with me. I believe that is absolutely ridiculous! Who in this world can guarantee that they will not have a medical condition ever? It meant nothing to the people in power that she wanted desperately to be with me. She is a young woman who is developing emotionally and physically and she needs her mom for obvious reasons.

It became so discriminatory (I hesitate to even use that word in fear of people assuming I am taking advantage of the term) that at first I was told that Sarah and I would only have visitation with each other. This would mean that she and I would only be together every other weekend and sometime during the summer until she was eighteen. That also would have given her dad the legal ability to make ALL decisions regarding her life.

My stomach felt like it dropped when I heard those words. I became physically ill the evening I received that news. In my mind, I dropped to my knees in anguish. The tears flowed from my eyes uncontrollably and my entire family grieved together joining in prayer to ask God for His direction and mercy. Persevere? How in the world could I even fathom a lifetime without my child? I was nauseous.

There were so many injustices that had occurred. My child was in pain and nobody would listen. Many times I had to fight the urge to scream! She would call me during the night crying hysterically for me to come and bring her to me. I felt so helpless. I cried out to God, "Why my child? Please, Lord, ease her pain."

It was eventually decided that my ex-husband and I could have a joint-physical care arrangement for Sarah. I am grateful that she and I can at least have time together. I try to count my blessings since I now am aware that statistically mothers with disabilities are always perceived as "less than" in a child-custody proceeding (although I know many women and men who raise their children beautifully with many varieties of disabilities). Even as I make additions and revisions writing some of these memories, I often have silent tears but I must remain focused on the many positives the Lord has provided in my life.

The divorce has been final since May 2011 and I have learned many things about our daughter, my relationship with my ex-husband during and after our marriage, and most importantly, myself. I may never know why these things had to occur for Sarah. It seems as if everybody got what they wanted from it except her. Her dad got away from his "obligations" as my husband and it appears that he is very happy. Although I could feel a variety of emotions towards him, I do not wish bad things for him. In fact, I need to focus on the fact that without each other neither he nor I would even be the parents of our beautiful daughter. Women with disabilities are generally not allowed to adopt by themselves and the same is true for single men. God once again knew what He was doing when he placed my ex-husband and me together in the same classes at UNI. He was preparing the way for both of us to have the honor of knowing Sarah.

I will always be grateful to God and admittedly my ex-husband for their parts in allowing me to be her mom.

I only hope he can find the life he has desired for so long and have a lifetime of happiness and fulfillment. I hope he can learn how to forgive me for my contribution to the end of our marriage. I desire these things because I realize that as long as he and I can set an example of grace and forgiveness towards one another our daughter will be the one who really benefits.

I am sure there were times when he felt as if my wheelchair received unnecessary attention by others and that he had to make certain sacrifices to be married to a woman in a chair.

I personally thank God that I have completely forgiven him for the pain that I felt during the end of our marriage. There are and will obviously be times in the future where we will disagree. That is what occurs when a family becomes broken. Unfortunately, the person who suffers the most is the one who was completely innocent during the entire thing - our daughter. Beyond that, I believe that the angels shed tears at the loss of what God designed: His family.

Emotionally, physically, and financially, I have lost many things since our troubles began. But I have gained one primary resource. I believe in myself. I am beginning to remember who that young woman was before my world changed. I am starting to acknowledge, once again, that I can love myself because the Creator loves me. That itself is a great place to start.

"Life shrinks or expands in proportion to one's courage."
Anais Nin

Chapter 21

Earthly Angels Don't Need Wings

〰〰〰

Luke 12:8

"I tell you, whoever publicly acknowledges me, the Son of Man will also acknowledge before the angels of God."

(NIV)

As I come to the conclusion of this memoir, I must mention certain people who've been my earthly angels. The first individual who deserves my honor and gratitude is my Grandma Thelma Hayden. Grandma, met Jesus on July fifth of 2011 and we all miss her dearly. Grandma lived a faithful and honorable life. Although her childhood was filled with uncertainty and fear, she maintained a sense of forgiveness and generosity towards others. She and Grandpa Gene did not have an abundance of worldly possessions but they were both dedicated to helping others with their service. I will continue to love and cherish our relationship by trying to follow her example of unconditional love for my family and her love for Jesus. Thank you, Grandma, for always being there for me and loving all of me. I love you and miss your physical presence but I know you are now in the room God prepared for you.

My next angel is a woman named Patty Biersner (Pat). Pat has been in my life consistently since June 2010; she was the first nurse that I met. Because of the physical and emotional stresses I had been under at that time, my health was so precarious that I needed home-health services. Pat has been a nurse at Covenant Medical Center for years and has been employed as a home nurse for many of those years. She has even been awarded as one of the number one accomplished nurses in Iowa. But above all things, she is a child of God who loves Jesus. Her uncanny ability to empathize and go above-and-beyond is no coincidence since she herself has battled the fear of death with illness. Her compassion and sense of humor are equally useful. She is a beautiful lady with a beautiful heart and I appreciate her for being a Christian example in my life. Thank you Pat for caring for me, Sarah, and my family. I love you and pray that the Lord will continue to bless you with health, joy, and continued unwavering faith.

I also want to bless my dearest friend whom I have known since we were twelve. Jacki Brucher-Moore has a knack for telling me the truth whether good or bad. She has known me so long that she vividly remembers things about my character and ability to cope sometimes better than I do. She knows I always try to keep everyone happy and not upset others, yet she is also aware of how defensive I can be. I love this woman!

My dear friend Marty (I consider her to be a mother-figure), who has known me since I was a young child. She is always taken the time to encourage and support me. Her witty sense of humor has been filled with wisdom and truth. I am so lucky to have her in my life.

Kathy Oakland, I cannot hesitate to mention you! Kathy works at the University of Northern Iowa as an educator and attends Nazareth Lutheran Church in Cedar Falls. She and I first met when I was an undergraduate in education in 1989-1994. Kathy and I remained in contact periodically throughout the years after graduation. We had not spoken in the past five to seven years until I came back to Cedar Falls in 2010. On the first Sunday in Cedar Falls after church, my parents and I went out for breakfast and here is how the conversation occurred:

Me: "Hi, Kathy. How are you?"
Kathy: "Ami!! How are you and what are you doing back in Cedar Falls?"

Me: "That's a loaded question."

Kathy: "Well, then let me ask you this, what
           have you been writing lately?"

Me: "Absolutely nothing; it's still all in my
           head. I've just been really preoccu-
           pied lately."

(In my mind, I was thinking divorce, pressure
ulcers, not being with Sarah, moving back with
my parents, etc. — nothing extremely positive)

Kathy: "Well, it's time to get motivated!"

And she handed me her UNI business card.

That was the beginning of this memoir and
the start of a student-mentor relationship
which I adore. I appreciate Kathy for her ability
to speak the truth about her fervent love of
Jesus Christ and her wisdom about life itself.
As I have gotten to know her on a more personal level, I have witnessed her selflessness
and desire to help others succeed. I thank God

for you, Kathy. I thank Him for putting you in my life twenty years ago. I am forever grateful for His design and His plan to allow me to know your kind and generous heart. I love you.

God has placed far too many individuals in my life at just the right time to mention, but I would be remiss if I didn't give a shout-out to some dear friends who have traveled along this road with me. My best friend from elementary school is a loving, sensitive man. David Gemoll has always played a big brother role in my life. We lived next door to each other and, as I look back, I think I may have actually had a little crush on him! This is so embarrassing to share with anyone, but I must admit it's quite hilarious now. Here is one particular scenario I can recall:

We were next door neighbors and all of the kids in our neighborhood liked playing hide-and-seek together. I usually liked hiding with someone (probably because I knew I was not a good runner or something), so I made sure this time that I hid with David. His family had two separate garages and in the 1970's and early 1980's, they were usually not connected to each other. We hid in between the garages behind a canoe. Smart, huh? It must have been his idea. I do not remember how old we were that summer, but I do remember that most of our mutual classmates who lived in our neighborhood had decided to partner-up for the summer as boyfriend and girlfriend couples. I am imagining we were probably in 4th or 5th grade. I don't know what forced these next words out of my mouth. It could have been the sweltering Iowa humidity or the fact that if everyone else had a boyfriend, then I wanted one, too!

Keep in mind that we were playing hide-and-seek, so we did not want to get caught. With a whisper, I said:

Me: "David?"
David: "Yeah?"
Me: "Do you want to kiss me?"

David: "No."

Me: "OK."

That was the end of our romance! I figure now (as I laugh at myself) that was God's way of allowing David and me to continue to experience a life-long friendship. He now lives with his wife Judy and their beautiful newborn son and her daughters. I am grateful for you David for always speaking your truth and beliefs. Thank you for being one of the constants in my life.

Another extremely supportive person in my life is my sweet friend, Deborah Warren. She and I met in 2007 when my ex-husband, Sarah, and I made our big move to the Greater Des Moines Area. Deb is the assistant to the Special Education Director in the school district Sarah attends. My ex-husband has been employed by the district since then, and I worked there in the 2007-2008 school year. Deb and I did not become close friends until my ex-husband and I started having problems and she has been helpful, intuitive, and supportive of my emotional and spiritual growth. Deborah is a wonderful woman and I have grown to appreciate her knowledge of Scripture and how it relates to our lives. Thanks, Deborah, for making it a priority in your life to nurture our friendship and future as life-long friends.

Lastly, there are a few women who I have known since college when we were Active Alpha Delta Pi Members at the University of Northern Iowa. I believe that as we get older (hopefully wiser), God gives us the ability to decipher through the good (and not so good) people whom we have met. I have been blessed enough in my life to have met wonderful Christian women through the Alpha Delta Pi house years ago. Because of our common beliefs in loyalty and being there (in whatever capacity we are able) for one another throughout the years, the following ladies have been a tremendous support system for me. I hope I can, someday, by my service and continued prayers, repay them for their kindness.

Kelsey (for talking to me all hours of the night on our cell phones); Molly (for stopping over for girl-talk and for coffee at Panera Bread when I know you're so busy and for helping me with this memoir); Sarah H (for your constant commitment to our friendship regardless of the miles between us); Traci (for praying for my emotional and physical healing); and Janet and Berta (for caring about Sarah and me via Facebook, although you have never actually met her).

The one thing that is true about all those people in my life (and the people in your life) is that He planned for them to be with us and to what extent from the beginning. He is a sovereign and all-knowing God!

"Real friendship is shown in times of trouble;
prosperity is full of friends."
Ralph Waldo Emerson

Chapter 22

I Will Serve

Proverbs 27:17

"As iron sharpens iron, so one person sharpens another." (NIV)

I recently heard about an old-Italian story which involves a homeless beggar. The poor man would walk to a beautiful, ornate church in Rome every day and visit a statue of an Italian Saint. He asked the statue for many years to help him win the lottery.

After years of hearing the beggar plead for help, the statue came to life. The beggar was startled, yet amazed, expecting the statue to hand him the winning ticket. To the beggar's surprise, the statue jumped down from his pedestal and replied, "OK, just go buy a lottery ticket!" This is obviously not a direction from God, but I got the point as soon as I heard it. We need to move to receive!

Although it's not a Biblical reference, it is relevant. Because we are children of God, it is required of us to be His servants. The more I realize this, the more I expect of myself. God has given me the gift of the desire to succeed. To me, this does not necessarily mean financial rewards or that the more I accomplish the more possessions I receive in return. As I have gotten older, my definition of success describes how I treat others and what I can do to serve them. Do not misunderstand me; I am just as selfish as most. In fact, my disability has played a part in my occasional belief that God owes me. Really, Ami?

Some of these thoughts in my mind have been assumed by me because of the unusual occurrences I have endured. I actually believed at times that they would eventually guarantee blessings. The "What About Me?" syndrome can be detrimental to our relationships and society. Our lives are a gift from God and we are responsible for not only leading others to Christ, but representing ourselves in a manner that serves Him, not ourselves. The coined phrase, "What Would Jesus Do?" actually should apply to all of us.

There have been too many times in my life where I have chosen to hear my words and desires, not His. It could be as simple as a decision like listening to music that is detrimental to my character or as serious as coveting my friends' marriages or finances.

This past year has been an atrocious year for me. I have never felt so lonely or abandoned in my life. There were even times when I experienced moments when I felt unloved by God. But as time goes on, I believe I have gotten a little bit wiser. I am trying on a daily basis to give grace to those who are hurting and therefore, unintentionally hurt me. I must remember that if His grace is overflowing and never-ending towards me, my loved ones, and even my enemies, then surely I can make an effort to do the same.

Because of the struggles in my personal life the past couple of years, the Lord has also placed a desire in my heart for service towards others. I am so grateful for that! He has provided me with a wonderful church where I have been reunited with old friends and church leaders. I have resources to draw from to accomplish this desire and goal. Orchard Hill Reformed Church in Cedar Falls, Iowa is filled with many enthusiastic, motivating individuals who inspire me to want to help others. My plans include starting a ministry where individuals with disabilities can find an environment where they feel accepted and loved by others. I know for a fact that Jesus put that thought and desire in my heart.

He has mercifully given me an exciting opportunity to go back to the University of Northern Iowa to receive my Master's Degree in Early Childhood Special Education. My Advisor

Donna Raschke actually attends the same church that I do and she introduced herself to me this summer to offer me a full-ride scholarship through a grant she had written. I have been going to classes since August 2011 and will be forever grateful to her for giving me this gift. I am starting to find worth within myself and remembering that I am a contributing member in this world. I do not know where the Lord will lead me once I have received my degree but I know that more doors will be opening, more opportunities to financially provide for Sarah, and most importantly, my life has and will continue to have meaning. I feel very blessed.

As a follower of Him, I must continue to read the Word daily, surround myself with people who encourage my Biblical beliefs, and listen when He speaks to me. This has been a concern that I have struggled with my adult life- knowing if it is God speaking or me. That is why I must know scripture and apply it to my decisions and thoughts. I must admit, however, that I am not as learned with scripture as I would like or need to be. A personal goal of mine is to study and soak it all in so I can refer to it in times of my challenges, joys, and fears, and to be able to help others when they need a little "boost" from God.

I am making a promise to myself, Sarah, my family, and the Lord to no longer wait for good things to happen, but to allow the Holy Spirit to motivate my actions. If I listen to Him, He will lead me in the right direction.

"If you don't set a baseline standard for what you'll accept in life, you'll find it's easy to slip into behaviors and attitudes or a quality of life that's far below what you deserve."
Anthony Robbins

Chapter 23

(2011-2012)
His Timing

〰〰〰

Isaiah 46:10

"Only I can tell you the future before it even happens. Everything I plan will come to pass, for I do whatever I wish."

(NLT)

Remember when I wrote about my amazing family and how much they all mean to me? Within the last few months, my mom's kidney which is in my body has finally taken the road to its last days. At this time, my kidney function is only 9% and I can once again sense the fatigue associated with the loss of function. I am assuming that the toxins in my body are literally attacking my bloodstream since the kidney is one of the main bodily organs which removes waste from the blood. As I write these words, I am remaining hopeful for my health to once again be restored because my beautiful sister Beth. She has agreed to be my next donor. Now, as far as our family is all concerned, this in itself is only because God's plan has proven to once again be bigger than anyone can fathom. Who would have ever known that when we became a family in 1982 she would end up being the same blood type and tissue match as me today in order to save me from a lifetime of dialysis and potential death? This is another example of His ability to see all things until the end of days.

Thank you Beth for your sacrifice for me so that I can live a longer, healthier life with Sarah and those I love. Thanks to Scott, her husband, for praying with your family and coming to the agreement to support Beth in her choice to undergo the surgery. I will never be able to adequately repay your family's sacrifice, but my heart will be forever grateful to you.

"Never think that God's delays are God's denials. Hold on; hold fast; hold out. Patience is genius." Georges-Louis Leclerc

A Letter from a Leader of Orchard Hill Church:

Every life is a unique and memorable story. As I've read the pages of this book, my heart has been touched by the thoughts and experiences within Ami's story. I've found places within her story that connected with my own story and events that increased my awareness of a story different from my own.

I was touched deeply by her love for her daughter. I was emotionally moved by the loving support of her family during both the good and challenging times. I was humbled by the vulnerable sharing of this single mom finding her way through a journey of disease and single parenting. I was encouraged by vivid memories of grandparents who cared enough to show up again and again.

I was challenged by Ami's recollections of the many times she reached out and prayed for God's help. I reflected upon the challenges that she has faced from which my life has been spared. I was grateful that Ami has shared her story with us.

I hope that when you read these pages that you sensed the holiness of this story. I hope that you found connections between her story and your own. I pray that your own awareness of God at work in your story will be enhanced as you read of God's work in Ami's story.

Dave Bartlett

"Stronger"

Hey, heard you were up all night
Thinking about how your world ain't right
And you wonder if things will ever get better
And you're asking why it is always raining on
you
When all you want is just a little good news
Instead of standing there stuck out in the
weather

Oh, don't hang your head
It's gonna end
God's right there
Even if it's hard to see Him
I promise you that He still cares

When the waves are taking you under
Hold on just a little bit longer

He knows that this is gonna make you stronger,

stronger

The pain ain't gonna last forever

And things can only get better

Believe me

This is gonna make you stronger

Gonna make you stronger, stronger, stronger

Believe me, this is gonna make you...

Try and do the best you can

Hold on and let Him hold your hand

And go on and fall into the arms of Jesus

Oh, lift your head it's gonna end

God's right there

Even when you just can't feel Him

I promise you that He still cares

Cause if He started this work in your life

He will be faithful to complete it

If only you believe it

He knows how much it hurts

And I'm sure that He's gonna help you get

through this

When the waves are taking you under

Hold on just a little bit longer

He knows that this is gonna make you stronger,

stronger

The pain ain't gonna last forever

In time it's gonna get better

Believe me

This is gonna make you stronger

Mandisa

What If We Were Real—2011

I Surrender to You, Lord

Dear Heavenly Father,

Thank you, Lord, for being my best friend. I want to give you thanks for giving me the joy and security of faith in you during my lifetime. You have always loved me and been my 'go-to' for advice and my reality checks in life, Lord. You remind me that perception is not reality, but your word is reality! Even in these times of the unknown, loneliness, and despair, you guide me to turn to scripture. You refresh my desire to serve you by serving others.

Lord, I do ask You to bless my life by showing me how to start fresh, be confident in whom You made me to be, and stay focused on the biggest goal in this world: bringing others to know You as their personal Savior. I need You, Lord, for every aspect of my life:

I want to acknowledge and always praise you for Your mercies and the grace you have given me in order to make it in this world. You are the one and only reason I am here in the first place and I vow to honor who you are.

God, I know that I will continue to sin and face the consequences of those sins. I know that when I ask you for forgiveness, I will be forgiven instantly. But, Jesus, please help me to forgive myself as well. Remind me that you died on that tree for me and that You do not want me to carry that burden within my heart.

Please, God, bless my daughter in making choices that honor You and who You created her to be. Constantly remind her that You are and always will be her light to follow. The darkness in this world can be tempting for many people, yet with You, her salvation is guaranteed. Jesus,

I realize that You love her even more than I do. You brought us together in this world because Your plan for her is greater than anyone can fathom and I'm grateful for You. Thank you for giving me the joy of being her earthly parent and for the memories you have allowed us to create together in the past and in the future. Guide her, Lord, and when I have come to join you in Heaven, reassure her that I loved her from the moment I saw her!

God, you are my provider. Help me to surrender everything to you. Remind me that my life is worthwhile in spite of negativity I have heard from those in my life whom I thought I could trust with my safety and future. I need your guidance in not only saying that you are all-knowing, but living those words, because you know my pain and fears in this world. You are my Lord and Savior.

Thank you for my life, Jesus.
Because of you, I am stronger.

CPSIA information can be obtained at www.ICGtesting.com
Printed in the USA
BVOW021134250312

285956BV00002B/6/P